To My Old Master and Chief

CONTENTS

ILLUSTRATIONS

HENRY IRVING

HENRY IRVING

PROLOGUE

HENRY IRVING was born in 1838 and died in 1905.

The book I wanted to write on this very remarkable being, I wanted to be perfect. This is far from perfect, still it is the best that I can do. I hear from afar the quiet, dear voice of my old master, ever critical and kind, saying: " Hmm — it's a pity the young man's best is so bad! "

This " young man " who is writing here is well over fifty, and though he entered the service of Irving at the age of seventeen (in 1889), he is now what he was then, a young man in so far that his heart feels just the same young affection for his old master as it did in 1889 . . . and has added some understanding to the affection.

All pupils are so, but some prefer to disguise their feelings. I have for long attempted to postpone, and postpone indefinitely, making any record of my master, for the reason I have given. It is a creditable reason, and is one which curbs most disciples or pupils, and in good time curbs them.

But I am off. Let me state at once, in clearest unmistakable terms, that I have never known of, or seen, or heard, a greater actor than was Irving.

This first crow as challenge, and as salute to the sun. I hear, from all the hill-tops, answers coming back from other reckless fellows who strut up and down their own runs, crying: "Cock-a-doodle-doo! We too have seen the sun!"

Well, then, we are all agreed. The sun's the sun. Our opinion is our opinion and, what is more, we have in us a certain something spoiling for a fight about it all.

We are not concerned with any of those fellows who would like to argue the point. We have no time to wait until their talk has driven the sun down and plunged us all in the dark.

We are concerned with the other thing — the sun rising, the curtain rising, the excitement which lies in the words: "I am going to see Irving in *The Bells!*"

It is two o'clock, and the play doesn't begin until eight o'clock, nor will Irving, dressed as Mathias, be at the door which is so suddenly flung open, until fifteen minutes past eight. But we know what we are going to get, and when it comes it will beggar our expectation.

So that is why I abandon myself to the old joy, and here throw all self-conscious logic and egoism to the wind and become once more spectator and whole-hearted admirer of this exceptional actor, Irving.

*   *   *   *   *   *

> *I wish they wouldn't make such a white-winged angel of father. He was never that.*
> — LAURENCE IRVING

Laurence Irving's wish is a good one. He hates the white wings of sentimentality. So do we all, but though I would clip the wings, I wouldn't add to the figure a beak and claws. How to satisfy this son is the question

—how to do it without making the father seem de-moniac? Not to make him out to be a saint is easier said than done, and for the life of me I can't make him out to be anything else.

For what is a saint and what an angel? Is every saint made of nothing but righteousness? Amongst duffers, yes, but have duffers a monopoly in *all* the best saints? Have no saints been left over for the rest of us? If so, I know that our saints look and act just like Henry Irving. As for angels — angels wink and smile, and angels are hard. One need only read a line of William Blake to be reminded of this. Irving was an ironical saint — a masked angel — with an eye for *réclame,* but not at the expense of his friends — such an important point — with two eyes in his head for his work, and his heart in the right place and quite unspoiled, for humanity. And if this generation does not know him more intimately, maybe it is because he refrained from writing his memoirs.

Memoirs are written presumably so that the world may take one at one's own estimate — see through the cloud of language — get at one's real thoughts and feelings by the way one writes of others — and some memoirs are written to make money.

Irving, according to the gifted authoress of *My Sentimental Self,* was to have written his *Memoirs.* "It was," she writes, "*Irving's intention, after he had completed the two years' farewell tour, to go back again to Tintagel, engage the rooms where he had spent so many contented weeks, and write his memoirs, which an enterprising American had failed to encourage earlier, even with an offer of a preliminary fee of five thousand pounds."*

There is something of Irving in that — for surely only a saint would have withstood the pretty temptation of £5000.

HAD Irving published his memoirs, it is probable he would have employed someone to write them for him. While he lived, his friend and secretary, L. F. Austin, wrote many of the lectures which have been handed down to us as by Irving. Actors really are busy people, and have little time to cultivate the art of writing — and Irving, always a stickler for form, liked L. F. Austin's style. Irving's *Memoirs* would have been stately, not spontaneous, although he had a great admiration for that which is spontaneous. He would have seen to it that nothing offensive to others appeared in his book and, as he was no Mrs. Bellamy or Mrs. Baddeley, there would have been " no scandal about Queen Elizabeth." Yet these are two instances of theatrical *Memoirs* which were a great success, and which purported to be by Mrs. B. and the other Mrs. B., and were no such thing.

To accept them as such, we would have to see the manuscripts in their own handwriting. No such MSS exist.

Both were compiled by a grub named A. Bicknell. Sophia Baddeley was " a very beautiful woman with a very bad character . . . she became very popular as an actress but her *amours* are more interesting than her acting. She died, a prey to drink, disease, and want, about the year 1784." George Anne Bellamy was " a noted actress whose private history is of rather a sensational order. . . It is of no value theatrically."

And so it is often with these big personalities who appear on the boards of a stage, who are lured on to write their *Memoirs*.

What have these two biographies to do with Irving's promised but unpublished *Memoirs*? This — that we needed some first-rate example, some standard — and all we have in place of that are these two famous *Memoirs* by Sophia Baddeley and Mrs. Bellamy. For neither Garrick nor Kean, Mrs. Siddons, Rachel, or Talma, wrote their *Memoirs*. Macready kept a diary, a seemly sort of thing, sometimes valuable to the historian, but decidedly gloomy — and one or two of the lesser lights, Young, Cooke, and poor Everard, have left uninteresting records. Sophie Arnould had a project of writing her reminiscences, and tried to lure the Comte de Lauraguais into a collaboration: but we have to thank both her and him that she changed her mind.

It was his unexpected death which robbed us of the book by Irving — and no one was rascal enough to rout out some of his notes and write it up and issue it after his death, as coming from him.

Since Irving has not left us his *Memoirs,* some of us have written little notes telling what we remember of him.

I could write a good deal more that I remember — such as of the time he smacked the prompt book out of the hands of the prompter during a rehearsal; of his amazing patience with a young actor who failed to remember his part; of his full opinion of Mr. Bernard Shaw; of his generosity to his company and staff, and of a hundred other little personal things known to me — either because witnessed by me, or because I possess a box-full of his letters.

But what are all these? Tell the story of the prompter with sufficient bias — and I can set all London cackling tomorrow with the tale.

We all have plenty of material to embroider on, whomever we come to write about, but one needs the nature of a malicious valet or soured lady's maid to dream of doing so — and some of their vindictiveness, to do the thing quite brilliantly. Yes, I see how I could make a black-winged demon of Irving by embroidering an insignificant fact with a devil of a lot of lies.

THE END OF A TRADITION

It is now twenty-five years since Irving died, and today I have a reason for writing this little book.

The reason is that perhaps there are young men of twenty-five years of age who would like to know something of a remarkable man, and who would be glad to hear it from one of his pupils.

To those who have reached thirty years of age, it will also come as something fresh, because at the age of five they can hardly have been allowed to go to the theatre, and if one had chanced to see him in the last year of his life, in that year, 1905, one would have seen him when excessively tired and not at all himself.

Then there are still others who were seventeen years of age at that time, and are now forty-two, and who did go to see him, let us say in *Dante* at Drury Lane, and, maybe, did not think very much of him — not only because he was tired, but because the play was not particularly good — in fact it was particularly bad — and because all that time, Irving, like any great actor, was only able to play magnificently those parts which he had created when a younger man; and this *Dante* was a poor thing, and prepared by him in his sixty-fifth year — and prepared in Drury Lane Theatre, a theatre strange to him — not his old Lyceum workshop. It is difficult to work in any but your own theatre, when you look on it as your very home.

7

Irving was fifty-one years of age when I, a very young man in my eighteenth year, came to perform for the first time at the Lyceum Theatre, under his direction. But it was nine years earlier that I first saw Irving — it was in 1880. I was then eight years old, and was taken to the Lyceum Theatre, not to see the play, but to grow a little familiar with the stage of a theatre during a performance of a melodrama. The reason I was not taken to see the play was that when I was a child I was very highly-strung — hearty enough — more often gay than glum — but subject to impressions more than most hearty children. I am told that a clown in a circus, balancing on a slack wire and pretending to fall, once sent me off into something like hysterics. I did not understand jokes which seemed to be dead serious things — and a melodrama full of delightful blood-curdling incidents was considered to be something I had best wait a few years to see.

So it was from behind the scenes of the Lyceum Theatre, from the O. P. corner, that I caught my first glimpse of Irving.

I was walking along in the dark, holding on to the hand of my guide, my mother, who was thrilled to feel that I was again behind the scenes of our home — the theatre. The first time I had been on a stage was when, in 1878, I appeared with my mother at the old Court Theatre, Sloane Square, in *Olivia*. I was on in the first act, amongst the villagers who crowd the scene — I was six years old. So when my mother who had joined Irving at the Lyceum in 1878, brought me to sniff the mountain air of the stage in 1880, it was so as to get me a little more used to the

Pit entrance to the Lyceum Theatre, about 1803.
No. 354 in the Strand.

giddy heights, the mysterious glamour, the strange darkened realms of the place. I don't recall the day or the setting out to go to the theatre: they who write memoirs seem to recall everything — I cannot, and some of my readers will know I speak quite truly when I say that my perceptions registered only certain vivid impressions, and these were flashed on my imagination and took it captive.

So all I can recall is that I was walking along in the dark, holding on to the hand of E. T.[1] There was hardly a sound to be heard, only some quavering music; and there I saw a ghastly figure of a man with a red wound showing on the left side of his chest, and this figure was rising up from the stage floor, and gliding its way across the stage as it came up; and there too I saw H. I., with his back to it and to us, seated, and scribbling at a table. This was the end of the first act of *The Corsican Brothers*.

Till that moment I had always looked on the stage as a blithe sort of place, either where horses ran round in a ring, or where people laughed or burst into tears gaily, and brushed the tears away happily, and flung themselves from one side of the stage to the other — all done with the lights turned well up, and with a good deal of flutter and noise. But that was all over now — and so was the brief, terrifying glimpse I had of the darkened stage, the travelling ghost, and Irving; for my mother took me below, under the stage; and passing through a forest of wooden machinery, we came at last to a steep ladder staircase, ascended it — and arrived once more on the stage floor,

[1] Already we had begun the English habit of calling people by their initials.

on the other side of the big stage; and suddenly all the lights were up, and there, amidst a tremendous bustle, together with the sound of thousands of people clapping their hands — there H. I. stood, between the front curtain and the glowing yellow footlights, taking his call: and I, looking to the right and the left, behind and in front, still holding on to E. T.'s hand, went off with her to the stage door, and out into the street and its cold mauve daylight.

The next time I saw H. I. was in 1882, again at the Lyceum Theatre, and again from the O. P. corner; then I saw the curtain rise on the brightly illuminated first scene of *Romeo and Juliet*. As I can recall one or two things about *Romeo and Juliet* at the Lyceum, I must have gone down to see it several times — maybe in a box, or maybe behind the stage. I recall meeting F. R. Benson — he played *Paris* — and I remember hanging by his hair: this he let me do to show his athletic powers — strength of neck — something or other. I remember the production which followed — *Much Ado About Nothing* — and three more of the productions which followed these two: and in 1889 I learned that H. I. was called "the Governor."

Until then he had been "Henry." I had heard him spoken of as "Henry" by his friends, and he had signed himself in letters to me, "Henry"; I have two in front of me at this moment — "*Affectionately yours, Henry*"; now what an extraordinary thing — for I can barely remember him today as "Henry" — only as master of the Lyceum Theatre — as Henry Irving. And that, of course, is as I like it to be.

The first letter is dated 1886 and was written on my

birthday, at The Grange, Brook Green, Hammersmith, and consists of these few words:

" Make good use of your time, for fast time flies," therefore spend this sovereign as quickly as possible.— Henry.

and I see that the piece of paper has been folded up into twelve; therefore, the sovereign was evidently wrapped up in it. The quotation is from *Faust* . . . the English version by W. G. Wills.

If anybody is curious to see what I looked like at that time, they will find me in a group photographed on board the *Arizona,* in which we came back from America in 1885. My mother and Irving had gone on their second tour to America in 1884, and my mother, feeling homesick, had cabled to someone in England who was going out to America, to " Bring one of the children." It wasn't that she didn't care which, only that she cared too much for both, and couldn't decide which was to be left behind. It was like that always. If I was given a cart, my sister was to have a horse and, giving these presents, she was ever fearful lest she should put the cart before the horse. I think she prided herself on being just, but with her, justice was almost an unknown atom in the sea of her love. She . . . but it is of Irving I am writing now, and as usual she and the rest of us give way before him — remembering too his peculiar antipathy to any crush, any unnecessary chatter about nothing which much matters. We didn't matter much, so we won't matter here.

Irving to me, at that time, was not an actor, but a very dear figure, sometimes appearing here, sometimes appearing there, generally bestowing a gift; in no way connected with thought in my mind — for I think I had not a thought in my head — but connected with vision, feeling. I had no notion of work in those days — I really did not know what it meant to work — which, by the bye, was a very great mistake of my nurse: a boy should begin to work when he is about three or four years old — then by the time he is thirty he won't make such a fuss about it, he won't feel that he has lost such a terrific lot of time.   But you see, so it is; when a mother has worked since she was five years old, she says to herself, very illogically, but with overmuch joy, " My children shall not work until they have passed their tender years " : and so I had the devil of a lot of time on my hands, and this very bad tuition of Irving, with his sudden appearances from nowhere, saying sepulchrally, " Make good use of your time, for fast time flies, so run off and waste this sovereign as quickly as possible " — really that was no way to educate an impressionable and tutorless youth of about fourteen years old.

I have been spending that sovereign " as quickly as possible " ever since, and I never found it grow a bit larger or smaller — it seems to have remained just the same old sovereign.   Of course you cannot stretch a sovereign out very much: so that when one day some years later, after I had become a member of his Company, Irving arrived at our house, at number 22, Barkeston Gardens, Kensington, and brought with him a volume of Green's *Short History of the English People,* of which a new edition was being published in parts at the time, price a shilling a part, and which was profusely illustrated; and when he let me get hold of it for a few minutes, and saw me devouring it with my eyes, he said, "I suppose you'll get the parts of this remarkable work as they come out." To purchase books was something which had never occurred to me, for my mother gave me any book she thought I might fancy. Besides this, although I was receiving £5 a week from Irving as a young actor, and the possession of money meant nothing whatever to me — I did not realize what money was for — I could not rapidly bring myself to contemplate spending a shilling a week on this sumptuously illustrated version of Green's *History* — and I said as much . . . my nurse had seen to it that by the time I had reached eighteen I was still about twelve.

Irving then gave me the second piece of advice. He said that he thought that out of my £5 a week — "You — er — get, I believe, that sum — er — weekly" — I ought to be able to afford some books. Well, I got some books at once; I got some more pretty soon after; I ran deeply into debt over books; and now I have about eight or ten thousand, and I'm still going on at it — but I wonder whether it was a good thing to do.

All the advice which Irving continually gave me in the course of my early career, I consider the very riskiest advice which you can give — if you judge by the usual way people advised us all when young: but there is only one thing I regret about it, and that is that he didn't give it to me earlier. I should like to have gone onto the stage to earn my living at the age of eight, instead of being "looked after," and a futile attempt made to educate me. Being put to work is the way my mother was brought up —

and Edmund Kean, and a host of actors, painters, musicians, and other good artists, great and small. They learnt no Greek or Latin, knew nothing of mathematics, some could barely write and read — and this made all the difference to them — it helped to keep them ignorant of a hundred thousand things, the knowledge of which would have certainly distracted them, and possibly would have prevented the painters from painting, the musicians from composing their songs. Artists are not to be educated in the same way as are sensible people, and therefore it is a waste of time to attempt to do so. That they can be trained for artists by being taught the crafts is another thing, and that is just what did not happen to me. So that when I first came to appear at the Lyceum Theatre, while I could speak a little German, and had won a prize in mathematics (to which I hadn't the faintest right), and knew something about William Blake, Rossetti, and circus hoops, I knew nothing whatever of acting or of the Theatre — though I had it in my bones.

All I knew was that Henry was vanishing slowly down through the floor, just as I had seen the ghost come up through it, and in his place was a person who looked through me — no longer saw me — was occupied with a hundred other things and a hundred other people; and I don't know that I liked the theatrical profession so very much after all.

I stayed in the Lyceum Theatre from 1889 to 1897, so that for eight years I saw Irving in most of his parts, and at nearly all the rehearsals of these years.

Rehearsing, at that time, was not controlled by the

clock, or checked by any Workers' or Actors' Union, as it is today.   Rehearsing in Irving's theatre was long and thorough, and I believe that we actors were not paid during the time necessary for our preparation.   Yet Mrs. Stirling, a very old lady in 1882, when she rehearsed and performed the part of the *Nurse* in Irving's production of *Romeo and Juliet,* was always " groaning out that she had not rehearsed enough " — so writes my mother in her memoirs.   What Mrs. Stirling meant was not that rehearsals were too few or too short, but that Irving seemed to her to be giving too much attention and too much time to the sceneries, the lighting, the orchestra, and the other parts of the jig-saw puzzle known as " production."

Irving was one of those men who consider that if a thing is worth doing at all, it is worth doing well — and he was not blind about the production of a play.   He saw that it consisted of a good deal more than the average actor of that day supposed.   The average actor held that provided the ten or fifteen chief actors of the piece were rehearsed over and over again, the music, the sceneries, lighting, and costumes, would take care of themselves — the actors never realized to what use these accessories could be put.   They felt about these things as do those men and women who at table are indifferent whether there is a napkin or no, whether a plate is hot or cold, whether the wine has been iced or warmed — the meat tough or tender — or the table-cloth clean.   The production of a dinner is not at all unlike the production of a play — taste, and much care for what seem to be unessentials, are necessary.

Here let me pause for a moment to ask you to get out

of your head altogether the notion that what I relate of Irving and the Lyceum Theatre was typical of the times. It was typical only of Irving. No one thought of the stage as he did: no one felt about it that it should be reformed altogether: only Irving determined to reform it as much as one man possibly could do, while producing plays year in and year out.

Try, then, to allow yourself to be persuaded by me to conceive of something very extraordinary, lest my words, which must be as plain as possible, convey to your mind something such as may be seen today, in any theatre, at performance or at rehearsal, and you inevitably receive the wrong impression. It can be seen in such a theatre as Stanislavsky controls in Russia — or Reinhardt in Germany — and it was seen in Sarah Bernhardt's theatre — not in Eleonora Duse's.

Believe me when I tell you that these Lyceum days were exciting days. They were positively worth living, if you chanced to be a member of Irving's company, and they were a full education to a young man wishing to do well towards the stage.

Irving had broken with many a tradition, but he had not broken with the most ancient one of all — that of working untiringly.

It is something to work untiringly at fifty-one years of age — to be holding up not merely your own theatre, but the whole English stage; to be giving it its direction, and to be ahead of it all the time; to be producing Shakespearean plays, one after another; and when not producing Shakespeare's plays, to be lending something Shake-

spearean to the other plays — for that is one of the things
that Irving did.

It is something to do all this, and it was something to
be in the midst of it, as I was.

I think that no one on the English stage will deny that
there is nothing today, in England, comparable with the
Lyceum Theatre under the rule of Irving.   I think there
are many who would like to see England with another
incomparable theatre.   After Irving's time, we opened the
flood-gates, and there has been a general inundation.   It
has done no harm.   After Irving should come a flood!

You will ask me why there should be a flood after Irving.
You may perhaps not be satisfied in your mind that there
was sufficient reason for it.   The reason is that Irving was
the end of a great line of actors.

He gathered to him all the old English traditions, he cut
away from those traditions all that was useless to him, and
then proceeded to display what was left, to exploit it further than it had ever gone before.   Then he blew it up!
The bits that came down were all seized on with avidity
and, on the strength of a chip, doubtless many of us
thought we were the old block itself.

That is what generally happens at the end of a great line
of tradition.   It was what Shakespeare did with the
Elizabethan drama.   After reading Shakespeare, it is
somehow not so good to be reading other Elizabethan
plays . . . it seems to us all much thinner.   It was what
Molière did with the French stage.   After *Le Malade
Imaginaire,* has been writ and played, it is best that

Frenchmen turn over a new page and try to start something else. There is always a new way — Nature and Art are not dried up, and the artist has only to go to Nature and Art and ask for a new map, in order to find a new way — but it is best not to go Shakespeare's way or on Molière's path, unless you can go further along them.

I do not mean to compare Irving with either Shakespeare or Molière, any more than I would compare these fiery particles with Vesuvius or Mount Etna.

What I mean is, that after any natural explosion, things are altered, and there will only be another when the time is ripe.

BRODRIBB

HENRY IRVING was born in 1838, down in Somerset, and
spent his early boyhood in Cornwall. His name was not
Henry Irving, because at that time he had not become
Henry Irving. His name was John Henry Brodribb.
Later on he became known as Henry Irving, as " Henry,"
as " H. I.," and as " the Governor."

When I say he had not become Henry Irving, you understand me to imply that he was what is called a self-made
man . . . yes, indeed . . . and in every sense of the
phrase. How he became Henry Irving, I will tell you later
on. Meantime, here we have a fine name for a farmer
. . . Brodribb. I daresay he would have dropped the
Henry if he had taken to the plough, and would have been
" plain John Brodribb, that have been here these eighty
year," etc. He was lucky to have lived in Cornwall and
in the midst of farms, that he might see for himself how
slowly things grow.

John Brodribb would have been the terror of the
neighbourhood if he had stayed down in Cornwall
. . . of that I have no doubt . . . for John Brodribb
had the devil in him. It was, as you will remember,
the thing that Voltaire begged that mild, lady-like Mlle.
Dumesnil to capture at all costs: " *Le diable au corps*
in all art if you want to obtain perfection," said he.

It was in Irving's case this *diable au corps* which led to the explosion to which I have referred. This fiend was troublesome to John Brodribb down in Cornwall, and so he went restlessly here and there, seeking to discover where — in what walk of life — it would really be most becoming. I do not know if you possess *le diable au corps,* whether you are an artist or no, in fact I am not sure whether it is necessary for an artist to be so unpleasantly possessed, but if you are an actor, or have leanings towards being an actor, you will know what I mean. You *must* have it. If it hasn't arrived, just go on until it does. To have *le diable au corps* will not profit you any, unless you know what to do with him when you perceive him perched, and croaking in your ear, " Nevermore! " I believe it takes people in different ways . . . one will groan . . . another will laugh, but an artist will blaze. It is this *diable au corps* which gives a tragic actor a capacity to blaze, and I think it is this same *diable* which allows a great comedian to laugh, and both these things are so pleasing to the general public. There must be often a satisfaction to the great performer, who, while is he performing, enjoys a happiness all his own. But when preparing to perform, the great performer is apt to suffer infernal torment through this same *diable.*

It was, I suppose, something of the strong Cornish farmer in him which lent Irving the power to control this demon during preparation hours, because never more than once in my life . . . in the life I spent at the Lyceum . . . did I see him in any way agitated, and I hold this to be

perhaps the most extraordinary thing that I know about
him.

Mortimer Mempes, who wrote a charming little booklet
on Irving, which he illustrated with some of his portraits
(none of which are like Irving) tells a story of Irving and
an old miniature-dealer, in the course of which he says:
"*Irving rushed into the picture dealer's and asked to see
the head of the firm. The son of the principal, seeing that
Irving was agitated . . .*" and so forth. Now Irving was
never *agitated . . .* Irving never *rushed* in any way. I
suppose he was the coolest actor possessing *le diable au
corps* that ever came upon this earth.[1]

Let me repeat that, after seeing them all, I consider him
the greatest actor of his time: not in England only, but
in Europe and America. He was also the most popular
actor of his day, both in England and America, but it was
in England and Scotland and Ireland that he was loved
most. He did not play in other European countries.

WHAT signify the words " personality " and " popularity "
to us today? Who in England today creates a wave
of enthusiasm wherever he appears? Of course it goes
without saying that the appearance of the King and Queen
of England, and the Prince of Wales, always arouses enthusiasm, but whether the British people today have the
same capacity for the expression of enthusiasm as they
once had, is another matter. You will be able to judge

---

[1] On December 4, 1880, Sir James Knowles, writing to Alfred Tennyson
about the preparations for *The Cup,* made the same mistake through the use
of the wrong noun — " Irving is in a great state of excitement, etc." *Excitement* is a word difficult to apply to Irving except when he was acting.

better than I, for I live in Italy. The only immense enthusiasm I have seen of recent years is that displayed by
crowds of men and women on catching sight of Signor
Mussolini. I mean that is the thing I call enthusiasm . . .
nothing less than that is worthy of the name. The feebler
thing, that "entusymusy"—which Lord Byron wrote
was the way Mr. Brahm used to pronounce it, and which
Byron called "cant"—that I do not mean. I mean the
glorious old article which, if it is not humming in London
today, will, we may be sure, hum again sooner or later.

Irving could arouse it, both in the theatre and out of it.
Out of the theatre it was controlled, in the theatre it was
frantic.

I think it has not been your fortune to hear what is
called "the house coming down." Even in the epoch of
Irving, it was seldom that anybody else "brought down
the house"—but Irving brought it down. A terrific
sweep of applause is not "bringing the house down."
"Bringing the house down" is when everybody simultaneously calls out and applauds simultaneously and elec-
trically. A vast number of people can ponderously express approval, but that is not what I mean.

You have been to the Russian Ballet, perhaps, on one
of its great nights, or you have heard Chaliapine's recep-
tion at Covent Garden. Well, that is not what I mean,
either. Those are ovations, but mild ovations. The thing
I mean had three times the capacity of that.

There is a picture in the Victoria and Albert Museum,
which I reproduce, and which shows us an English audience of a slightly earlier period, acclaiming the great

Her Majesty's Theatre, London, in 1841. Farewell of Mlle. Rachel at close of the 1841 season in June. Water color by Lami. *By courtesy of the Victoria and Albert Museum, London.* Remarkable for the courtesy of the public shown here (let alone its enthusiasm). From 1910 on the social section of any theatre public is prone to grab its programmes and run out of the playhouse before the curtain ceases rising and falling.

French actress, Rachel. Very like this was the spectacle in the theatre at the end of the Lyceum evenings.

And in the midst of this spectacle sat a number of men, grave, grieved, ridiculous. For what was there to be grave or grieved about? There they sat, next to Wilde, or near Mempes — in front of Mounet-Sully, or behind Paderewski — four artists enchanted with their evening, while the four critic-playwrights were disgruntled. Archer bewails — Bernard Shaw shakes his head — the *Athenæum* sneers, and the *Figaro* is glum. Enjoying nothing, anon they leave the theatre, to say that the audience were all fools suffering from Irving-mania. They say it in print, and they reveal what they do not say — they reveal an ignorance of all art — of all that is lovely, of all that is enchanting the judicious. They stubbornly "won't" — they hate the very thought of enjoyment and enchantment — "so there!"

We will come to them by and by: for the moment the sound of a tumult of applause is in our ears — "Irving is loved and appreciated" is the only thing it says, and the only thing which matters.

BRODRIBB PREPARES HIMSELF TO
BECOME HENRY IRVING

THE DATE when Brodribb set out to become Irving was when he set out to act in Sunderland, 1856: the date when he became Irving was fifteen years later, 1871, November 25th, when he acted and produced *The Bells*.

The artist begins his career on the date that he completes his masterpiece. There can be but one masterpiece, although we often hear of the thing in the plural. I had this from a connoisseur of pictures, who explained to me that a masterpiece was that piece of work done by a painter when his tutor had no more to teach him, and which entitled him to be called a master. This piece, *The Bells*, was Irving's masterpiece, and proclaimed him a master.

When Brodribb set out for Sunderland, he was eighteen and a half years of age. He had been denied the advantages of an early education, although in 1849, at the age of eleven, he was sent to the City Commercial School, off Lombard Street, over which ruled Dr. Pinches. It is said that at this time there were moments when he cared more for white mice than for learning. He left the school after two years, and was placed in the office of a firm of lawyers in Cheapside. He was only thirteen years of age. Then, two years later, happened to him what happened to the great French actors, Talma and Le Kain, when they were boys — he had a taste of amateur theatricals. By that

time he was fifteen years of age, and he was still Brodribb. This taste it was that made him hunger for the
stage. "Hunger," the only word for it, is a serious word,
and the serious happened.

Soon after this he saw Samuel Phelps act *Hamlet,* at the
old Sadlers Wells theatre; he also saw a play called *The
Haunted Man,* and another called *The Enchanted
Island,* at the Adelphi Theatre. What you taste and like,
you want. *Hamlet* and haunted men are what Brodribb
hungered to be; to "an Enchanted Isle" is where Brodribb longed to go. The stately, the weird, the impossible
. . . these three he liked, and they went with him to the
end of his days.

A year later, in 1854, an old actor of the name of William Hoskins, who was a member of Phelps's company, at
Sadlers Wells, gave him some lessons in acting, between
the hours of eight and nine in the morning — for soon
after nine, Brodribb was due at his desk in Cheapside.

Hoskins gave him a letter to a manager in Sunderland,
a Mr. E. D. Davis, and with this letter in his pocket, he
went northward in 1856.

Sir Squire Bancroft says that in the early part of his
career, Irving was by no means himself, that he had "*a
strong smack of the country actor in his appearance, and a
suggestion of a type immortalised by Dickens in* Mr. Len-
ville *and* Mr. Folaire."

On his first appearance at Sunderland on September
18, 1856,[1] he was urged by a critic in the morning paper

---

[1] Mr. John Parker tells me it was "September 29th" not "September 18th." The playbills give this date too. Irving gives the date as I give
it here. I feel sure Mr. Parker is correct and yet Irving cannot be wrong —

to take the first steamer back to his comfortable home, and to abandon all hope of becoming an actor. That critic was not George Bernard Shaw, but it is what Mr. Shaw would have advised, and he would have advised ill. Mr. Shaw was not in Sunderland at the time; he was helpless in his cradle, for he was precisely fifty-four days old. Mr. Shaw came later to London and did not fail to attack Brodribb (no one in his senses can attack Irving), because . . . but *" let me not name it to you, you chaste stars . . . it is the cause."*

I think that the advice of the Sunderland critic would have been followed by the actor, had he allowed himself for a moment to believe that it was John Brodribb who was going to become a great actor. But he knew better than that — he knew that it was his mask that was to be the great actor — a mask which could be a hundred faces in one — and he had to design, cut out, polish, and perfect that mask. This notion of being somebody whom you are not, does not find favour among all actors of today. Most prefer to be their natural selves, and I doubt whether any other actor has ever set out to transform himself so completely as did Brodribb. If the others were satisfied with themselves as they were, Brodribb was not self-satisfied. So that when the critics and the public advised him in a kindly way to give over, or hissed him from the boards, he took it well, not because of any contempt for their opinion, but rather because he agreed so heartily with their verdict. He would be Hamlet, the Haunted Man,

cannot be corrected by me, anyhow, until we change places and he becomes my pupil.

and he would sail for the Enchanted Island, and then we would see. Brodribb was never in a hurry: it is an old saying, I believe, that no gentleman ever is in a hurry, and although he believed that it would be a matter of three or four years ere he could become the Haunted Man, if not Hamlet, he was not put out by the discovery that it was taking much longer. On perceiving this, he did not change his direction; he went no faster — he only went more steadily on.

FROM Sunderland he passed to Edinburgh, playing there an astonishing number of parts in his two and a half years' sojourn. Those who wish to make quite sure that it was an astonishing number, should turn to the last pages of *The Life of Henry Irving,* by Austin Brereton (1908). There they will find that he played no less than 429 different parts in about 782 days — that is to say, more than a new part every two days. We are told by Mr. Brereton that this record has no parallel in the history of great actors.

The following were the Shakespearean parts given to him:

In *Hamlet*	*Guildenstern, Horatio, the King, the Priest, the Ghost, Osric,* and *Laertes.*
In *The Winter's Tale*	*Cleomenes, Florizel.*
In *The Taming of the Shrew*	*Hortensio, Biondello,* and *Petruchio.*
In *Romeo and Juliet*	*Paris* and *Tybalt.*
In *Richard III*	*Catesby, Henry VI,* and *Richmond.*
In *Othello*	*Cassio, the Messenger,* and *Montano.*

In *The Merchant*	*Salarino* and *Bassanio*.
of Venice	
In *Macbeth*	*Seyton, Ross, Banquo,* and *Macduff.*
In *King John*	*Philip, King of France.*
In *King Lear*	*Curan.*
In *Henry VIII*	*Earl of Surrey.*
In *Cymbeline*	*Pisanio.*
In *As You Like It*	*Sylvius* and *Orlando.*

He also played in the dramas of Sheridan and Gold-smith, and in a quantity of melodramas. At Christmas time, Pantomimes were put on, and in one of these, *Little Bo-Peep,* he acted the *Wolf:* in another, *Puss-in-Boots,* he acted the *Ogre,* and also a *Demon.* Brodribb as *the Wolf* must have been rather good — but what is more certain, Brodribb must have enjoyed himself vastly as the *Wolf,* the *Ogre,* and the *Demon.*

At the end of this Edinburgh experience he came up to London, and was engaged to play there, at Charles Kean's old theatre, the Princess's. But discovering on arriving that his part consisted of only half-a-dozen lines, he re-leased himself from this engagement, although it was an engagement for three years: and he left as soon as possible for Dublin, where he appeared on March 5, 1860, as *Cassio* in *Othello.*

He had gone to Dublin to fill a vacancy which had re-cently been created there. It appears that a Mr. George Vincent had been dismissed by the Manager, Henry Webb — rightly or wrongly, one does not know. But the gallery boys felt keenly that he had been wrongfully dismissed. This decided them, and Irving was greeted with a storm of hisses whenever he came on the stage. This lasted for three weeks. To undergo such an ordeal, *sangue freddo,* cold blood, is a necessity. I use the Italian words, because it is quite easy for cold-blooded people to be cold-blooded, but for hot-blooded people to keep cool is a very different matter. If you look at Brodribb's face, you will see that he is not exactly the type of the cold-blooded northerner. Had he been born in Venice he would not have seemed out of place. There was always just a slight resemblance between him and Novelli, the Venetian actor.

The words *sangue freddo* were being often used a short while ago by the Duce (pronounced *Doochy*), to call his followers to their senses. When they are insulted, they are to treat the situation in *sangue freddo*. It is a great blessing to have somebody calling you to your senses. It must be an invaluable aid to be able to rely on a voice which pulls you up and stiffens you to meet derision and insult. To do that for him, Brodribb seems to have had nobody. Twenty-two years of age, in Dublin, before the roughest public known to the northern world . . . "*There was I,*" he writes, " *standing aghast, ignorant of having given any cause of offence, and in front of me a raging Irish audience, shouting, gesticulating, swearing volubly, and in various forms indicating their disapproval of my appearance. Night after night, I had to fight through my part in the teeth of a house whose entire energies seemed to be concentrated in a personal antipathy to myself.*"

I have witnessed audiences behave like this in Italy, especially in Florence and Rome. They do not select an actor, as a rule. These goings-on are generally restricted to variety halls. It is not the comedians they deride, nor is it the acrobat. It is solely the young ladies — or old ladies — as may be — who are put on, for the first five or six turns, to fill in the bill. These women meet this awful attack courageously, showing utmost indifference, good-humoured jollity, or blazing despair — rarely this. It is "disgraceful" to badger performers, one knows that, and yet after all it is something of a compliment to have to perform before an audience that is not matter-of-fact and placid before what it somehow feels is excessively stupid, or if not excessively stupid, insipid and vulgar.

While listening to this crowd, I have often thought to myself, supposing a woman with a scrap of genius were to come on the stage, she would be able to silence them to such effect that they would end by cheering her to the skies. On the other hand, she would wake up, and anyhow learn something which no other teaching could give her. Yes, assuredly a rough crowd is a far better friend to the actor than a perfectly-mannered but malicious-tongued lot of ladies and gentlemen, apparently agreeable, but with little sympathy and no pronounced dislike — horribly polite. Faced with something that does not resist him, and expresses neither a *pro* nor a *con,* what on earth can the actor do? But faced with an audience up in arms, if he has the true spirit of the actor, he will get the better of it, and having done so, he will have strengthened himself.

This is what Brodribb did in Dublin. At the end of

three weeks, the howling and hooting ceased.[2] The
Manager was obliged to come on and protest that the
people in front were not playing the game; but I know
of few who would have stood three days of it, let alone
three weeks. It is perhaps permissible for Irishmen to
hoot an Irish actor, because I suppose an Irish actor would
know what it all meant, but to behave like that to a very
solemn young English actor of twenty-two is quite
another thing. But of course the gallery boys didn't
realize that three nights would have been quite
enough.

Like so many of the Italian girls hooted in Florence,
the Irish actor is doubtless quite indifferent to the cat-calls,
for to him it is a custom. One hears of scenes in Irish
theatres which seem to do no harm — Synge, W. B. Yeats,
and Lady Gregory have been cradled in them — and
their work is no worse for it, and maybe it benefited by
such experiences. Some Irishmen take it all, no doubt,
as a bit of fun, but Brodribb cannot have taken it as fun,
and this three weeks' ordeal must have acted on him like
a fire, as he stood there preparing himself to become
Irving.

As later on in life he never accepted the applause he received, so we may suppose that he refused to accept this
disapproval. .

How often have I and those who were in his theatre
seen him standing while the applause rained down like
a cataract, and he obviously there . . . bowing *so slightly,*

[2] Bram Stoker says the cat-calling lasted four weeks: a reporter in
Scotland quotes Irving as saying it lasted six weeks: Irving says three weeks.

to show that he was not only there, but aware; yet *never* accepting the applause . . . enduring it.

So then, while he was making his mask, in Sunderland, Edinburgh, and Dublin, he was at the same time measuring himself for a suit of mail which, when it should be ready, would cover him from head to foot: for indeed Irving was the nearest thing ever known to what I have called the Ubermarionette.

Now an Ubermarionette is all sorts of things at which I have hinted in books and drawings which I have made since 1907. I only hope that I have not wearied anybody with the notion of an actor who should be all that a marionette is and much more — and that I do not weary you now. But there is a point that I never touched on. It is a human point, and it is related to Irving, for from Irving the whole notion receives corroboration.

The actor is placed in a most difficult situation. He has to pass through some years of positive hatred from the public, who, if he succeeds later, will some years after come to the same theatre, and applaud him to the skies. How accept both of these insults? Irving is the only man I know of who knew how to do this. Aware, as I have said above, of the disapproval and of the approbation, he *accepted* neither the one nor the other. That is not human, is it? It is more than human, is it not? The human being will show that he is aware that he has been hissed or booed off the stage; he will show that he has been wounded. The human being who is damned will not appear very blessed, and the human being who is acclaimed by an approving or patronizing crowd, will also show that he has been touched. Yet it is the same human being, maybe the same actor, who has been hissed and applauded.

As Irving himself said, when speaking of Edmund Kean, "*The road to success lies through many a thorny course, across many a dreary stretch of desert land, over many an obstacle, from which the fainting heart is often tempted to turn back. But hope, and a sense of power within, which no discouragement can subdue, inspire the struggling artist still to continue the conflict, till at last courage and perseverance meet with their just reward, and success comes. The only feeling then to which the triumphant artist may be tempted is one of good-natured contempt for those who are so ready to applaud those merits which, in the past, they were too blind to recognise.*"

Now good-natured contempt is a very difficult thing to acquire. Will you not agree with me that it belongs to something a little more than human? For undiluted contempt is easy enough, and poisonous to him possessed by it. What is so difficult, is to mix with this poison that extraordinarily sweet thing, good-nature. The public, and indeed the critic, is apt to suppose that no actor or actress can be self-critical, for so few of them are that — but Irving was, I assure you, like all good actors, far more self-critical than any of his spectators. Let us not forget that he was a serious man; let us allow that there are other serious men working in the theatre today — actors, playwrights, stage-managers, and assistants — many of whom are to some extent self-critical. We may be sure that there will always be one who is more self-critical than the rest — one, therefore, who will never accept the criticism of other people, because it is impossible that they can estimate him as exactly as he can himself. Therefore, no artist who is self-critical, and at the same time a serious man, such as I have spoken of, can allow himself to abide by the verdict of the spectator or the critic. Praise or blame has indeed but a momentary effect upon the man whose discipline makes him a severe critic of his own works. So that when some writer, be he dramatic critic or theorist, separates the artist from the spectator, he is inventing a fantastic situation which is non-existent. For the artist is his own spectator and critic, ruthless and seldom quite just. Artists have, time out of number, destroyed their paintings, their essays, their poems. Some are doing so the very hour that you are reading this. Who can go further than that? We spectators assuredly cannot presume to teach such an artist. And the failure of the critic, who could help the artist and the spectators to come together, is, not to discern this kind of artist — or, having become aware of him and his self-criticism, not to proclaim him as the genuine thing, no matter what he does: for all that he does will be well done — and that's the man whose work we spectators want to see.

Unfortunately, the critic is quick to discern the man who is not like this, the confident, pretentious man, the man who believes that everything that he writes, everything that he paints, or every part that he acts, is perfect. Such a man inspires confidence in the critics. There are hundreds of such actors, and all they do is trivial. Yet their superficialities are trumpeted forth with confidence. No matter how vapid they are, the critics find them admirable. The public is told that it can with confidence be delighted. But I guarantee that if the young Henry Irving or the young Edmund Kean were to come onto a stage in London tonight, they would again be howled down as ridiculous, and damned by these critics.

As they were in their day — and shall be in every day to come. They always win in the end, yet were just as good when the people booed them as when finally they cheer them. So it comes to it that the only possible feeling that the triumphant artist may arrive at, is that which Irving recommended — *a feeling of good-natured contempt*. That was the suit of armour for which I said that this remarkable man was measuring himself, not for the defence of his person, but for the defence of the spirit of the artist.

Today no one hisses in an English theatre, at least so I am given to understand, so it might be as well that they should also cease applauding. It is only fair to the spectator that if he is privileged to the one expression, he should be at liberty to indulge both, and fair to the actor that he be spared both. When I was in Moscow, long before the Revolution, the best theatre was the Moscow Art Theatre, and in that playhouse there was neither applause to be heard, nor sounds of disapproval. Mentioning this in England, I was assured that it was impossible, that no actor could act well without applause. I noted at the time that nothing was said about the other thing, about hissing. But it stands to reason that, if a cheer is an incentive, a hiss is no less so. For as the now over-popular William Blake once remarked, "*Damn braces, bless relaxes,*" and certainly if you petted the members of the Royal Artillery for a week before an engagement, they would fall to pieces when the test came.

I wonder if something quite different, some other sounds from the front of the house, sounds which are neither filled with animosity nor choked with disgust, nor yet layered with something sickly, I wonder if such could not be devised — not by the brain of man, but through the combined pulses and stamina of a people. Some expression of the appreciation of its heart and mind — some under and deeper sympathy — no sentimentality or nervous gigglings — something real and good. I have felt this something in Italy, and I have felt it in no other land. It is both coarse and delicate. The two things, approval and disapproval, seem to cease their quarrel in a theatre, and become receptively attentive and expectant with an expectancy that can be felt.

I have hated the word " excitement," ever since I discovered that my own people disliked it.

What use to us is this word, if, when we use it, our friends take us to mean something emotionally superficial? But if we may use it here once more in a good old solid sense, then I would say that the spectators have to be excited. I was excited at the age of twenty-five, on going to the Lyceum to witness *The Bells,* and I know that many men, twice as old as myself, were excited too.

But there was quite a little of the other thing, the deadly

cynical or sentimental egotism, in that theatre. Not so much as there is in theatres today, but a good deal of it.

What that other thing is, I am quite unable to express better than I do here, but it is the thing which has ruined the British stage for a time. It is not entire indifference, because it buys its tickets; it arrives in time — or six minutes late; it talks loudly; is uncertain what it is going to see, or whom; it knows it is at a theatre even as a man knows that he is drunk, and proud of it — he can't get out of it at once, but forgets all about it when he does get out.

It was the presence of this thing at the Lyceum Theatre which caused a William Archer, aided by a Robert W. Lowe, to concoct a booklet called *The Fashionable Trage-dian*. This booklet was made in 1877, and its cynicism was directed at Henry Irving. How strange that the tittle-tattle of the public can so poison the mind and cripple the will of good men like Archer and Lowe, and cause them to commit so stupid a blunder. For the whole book reveals the fact that the good Archer and the good Lowe were unaware that the man bowing before the three thousand spectators was filled with good-natured contempt for that public, and that he was a great British actor, and not a charlatan. They mistook his attitude for one of servility, or they would not have written that book. And even as Archer and Lowe misunderstood, so do critics today misunderstand too many great artists.[3]

---

[3] Brereton says in his *Life of Henry Irving,* that " *some six years later, one of the authors, Mr. William Archer, recanted — in part — for some of his remarks in this brochure.*" I have not seen any such disavowal — neither did Mr. Archer reveal any signs of special illumination in anything he wrote later about Irving. Mr. Lowe, on the other hand, some eleven years after the appearance of *The Fashionable Tragedian,* wrote of Irving that he was " *cer-*

It is because of this that we need a different spirit in the spectators at the play, if the British Theatre is to recover its old good health. For the critics won't help — they are not noble enough — only the public can do so, by realizing its duty and its privileges.

But one must not be sweeping about dramatic critics, any more than about artists, for some critics are fine artists, and these are self-critical too. In my younger days there was a noble critic, ever ready to praise a good artist no one else had marked, and his name was Arthur Symons. There was an old dramatic critic — old Davenport Adams — another, E. F. Spence, then Haldane MacFall. And I think it is evident to us all that today a new race of theatrical critics is assuredly coming to the fore in England, alive to the value of the Theatre, and determined that it shall be a serious Theatre. We have only to recall the names of J. M. Bulloch, of Morgan and Swaffer, of Ervine — praised by all but me — of Walbrook, Darlington and Griffith, of Ellis Roberts and Desmond MacCarthy, to feel assured that dramatic criticism is in safe hands.

If I have digressed for a while, turning from the man of our moment to the thing itself, the Theatre, there is no one who would approve me more than Irving. For Irving was not all for himself. He wished the Theatre to go on to better things, and never to be a stick-i'-the-mud, doing

---

tainly the most remarkable actor of this generation, and the legitimate successor of Betterton, Garrick, Kemble and Edmund Kean" — and the same year, dedicated to him his Bibliographical Account of English Theatrical Literature — in my opinion one of the most valuable of books, and one I use daily.

as was done last time. If now he could walk into this room, he would say: "That's right, me boy. Speak about that. That's important. A lot of young people are coming along who should be helped." When I say that he would have addressed me as " me boy," I mean that is how he spoke in those days of long ago, and it is very difficult to get out of the old feeling that one is still the same age as when one heard the pleasant voice talking in good-natured but slightly contemptuous tones about the future.

But at the time I was speaking of, Irving certainly had a future before him, and I cannot remember a time in his career when he was unmindful of the future. To him there was always a future, and he never retired — he went on.

If anyone died — was laid to rest in Westminster Abbey, it was Brodribb — for Henry Irving, that shadow of a coming event, the Ubermarionette, is still living.

THE LYCEUM THEATRE

THE FIRST Lyceum Theatre had been built by the architect, James Paine, and opened May 11, 1772. It was small and was used for all sorts of purposes until 1794, when it passed into the hands of the composer, Dr. Arnold. He seems to have rebuilt it, but he could not get a licence, because the actors and managers of the two large theatres, Drury Lane and Covent Garden, had been critically sitting on the whole idea of having any Lyceum Theatre in existence; but when Drury Lane was burnt to the ground, on February 24, 1809, these same actors and managers found the Lyceum Theatre so convenient a place in which to shelter, that they stayed there and played there until their new Drury Lane Theatre was ready.

Although for many years the Lyceum Theatre seemed uncertain of any special reason for its existence, it became quite sure of this when, in 1871, Irving stood on its boards.

It had become a moderately large theatre by the time that he first came to play in it, and later on, in 1881, when he was lessee and manager, he enlarged and improved it so that it was transformed into quite a big playhouse.

The Lyceum possessed certain features which proclaimed it to be a theatre, even from the street. The Lyceum has preserved these external features: Drury Lane

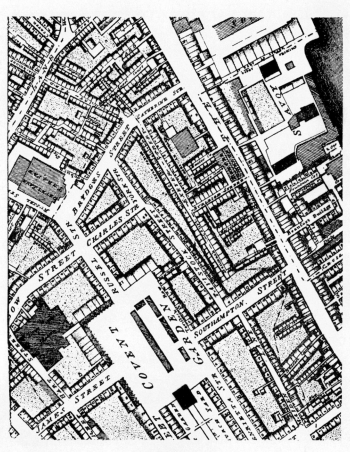

Showing place and position of the Lyceum Theatre 1792–99, and the proximity of Drury Lane Theatre and Covent Garden Opera House. The Lyceum was built in 1772; rebuilt in 1794–95, and again in 1834.

and Covent Garden and the Haymarket have done so too, while adapting their interior form to something new and strange, and not merely strange, but practical — if it be practical to disfigure a place for the sake of more pennies, to make more pounds at the cost of your life. The life of the theatre as a whole is of prime importance: of lesser importance should be the temporary excess profit of the shareholders, for if the whole theatre dies, these same shareholders suffer. Therefore, each theatre should preserve its best traditions, and one of these is that it shall always look like a theatre. For some reason unknown to me, it is not held to be so important nowadays for a theatre to look like a theatre, and it is sometimes difficult to tell one from a tea-room or a block of flats.

The main entrance to the Lyceum Theatre, in Wellington Street, does not hide itself away in that street, and does not pretend to be something it is not. As you pass along the Strand and glance up Wellington Street, you can see the Lyceum portico, with its six large pillars. While Irving was manager, the pillars seemed to be explaining that here could be seen and heard classical plays, and if you chanced to go by in the evening, you would see three large flaming torches, on the roof, which lit up the whole street with their flare. You may still see the flare, but it lights up nothing, shall we say, quite as good as it did in 1881.

The Lyceum had a better front than that of Drury Lane or Covent Garden, for it didn't sprawl, and the entrance was better for its flight of broad steps, which led straight up to the circles and from them down to the stalls; and it seemed to you all very theatrical and good, provided you could enjoy theatrical things like a hearty playgoer, and not reason about the unreasonable, like a pedant, till you thoroughly spoilt your evening.

As you passed from the street into this theatre, you found yourself immediately in a lofty hall, with the large staircase before you — not on one side, as at Drury Lane and Covent Garden. Entering most latter-day theatres, you discover yourself in a little square ante-room, like a modiste's parlour, and passing through insignificant door-ways, with notices about " Safety First," and other distracting information, you presently wend your way along well-lighted but narrow corridors, which remind you of all things except of a theatre. The Lyceum Theatre looked neither like the entrance-hall of your own house, nor like that of some wealthy neighbour — nor did it suggest that there hadn't been enough money to pay for the thing being large enough. It was what you might call an exciting entrance, as every entrance to a theatre should be. There are very few examples on record of any architect of merit ever having built a theatre without making his entrance to it as arresting as possible, and hinting of the wonders within, unless he has been baulked by lack of funds.

But, in 1871, in September, the month in which that excellent American manager, Colonel Bateman, opened the Lyceum, there appeared to be nothing arresting within. And yet, actually, young Brodribb was within — that is to say, Henry Irving, still held in leash by Brodribb.

Here we see an interesting situation. We see a bold American attempting to direct a large theatre in London: following his instinct and judgment by engaging this actor who was within two months of becoming the greatest actor of his age: and yet this astute and able manager (I had almost written, this dear old blunderer) hesitates to play this trump card which he holds in his hand.

The first reason for his hesitation is a very natural one. He is not thinking over-much of Brodribb—it is his seventeen-year-old daughter, Isabel Bateman, whom he is concerned about, and whom he wishes to see very famous. Very carefully old Bateman selects the play which shall bring them all renown, money, and happiness. It shall be a play on a celebrated story by Madame George Sand—*La Petite Fadette*. "Bound to be a colossal success," says Bateman. "And you, my dear," he adds, turning to his wife, "you shall adapt it as a play —Isabel shall play it — young Irving will do for *Landry,* and Georgina Pauncefort will be excellent as *Mother Fadette:* but we will call it *Fanchette,* not *Fadette.*" So he produced the said *Fanchette, or Will o' the Wisp,* at the Lyceum, on September 11, 1871: and, true to the ignorant old tradition that genius should ever support competent talent, Bateman gives Irving the small part of *Landry Barbeau.*

The play fails instantly. Does Bateman follow his original impulse, the impulse which made him take young Brodribb from the Vaudeville Theatre, where he had been playing *Digby Grant* brilliantly for over a hundred nights, with immense success — the impulse which made him exclaim: "That young man should play *Richelieu*"? Does he give him *Richelieu* to play? No. He acts as every theatrical manager does: he thinks for himself instead of trusting to the artist, and so he blunders again and again.

He took off *Fanchette* and put on an adaptation of *The Pickwick Papers*. The actor whom he had engaged for *Richelieu* — Irving — was put on to play *Alfred Jingle,* and of course he did so with praiseworthy success, but the play, a little bit of nothing, was not a success. And even after these two failures of September and October, even then the courageous but daft, if dear, old Bateman, even then the far-seeing man who had engaged this actor of genius, failed to see what it was he should do, and he positively purposed leaving England, to wander in America!

It was at this moment that Irving managed, somehow or other, to have a version by Leopold Lewis of *Le Juif Polonais,* called *The Bells,* put into rehearsal, "against Mr. Bateman's wish," says Irving . . . and the company of actors thought that Brodribb was quite mad.

The biographies of Irving all tell us of the deep depression under which the entire company, from Mrs. Bateman, through Miss Bateman, and down to Hawes Craven the scene-painter, all laboured during the twenty-six days that they were preparing this piece under an actor who was to change the face of the English stage.

It would almost seem that a state of deep depression is the desirable one for the English stage to enter before accomplishing something. But it may be suggested that

that moment is the very moment to do something crazy: it will not be misunderstood if I add that by this I mean something which *appears* to be crazy. For suppose that Bateman had done something safe and reasonable at the Lyceum in October 1871; suppose that " wise counsels " had prevailed; let us put it that " discretion and sound common sense " had prevented anyone from losing his head (you know what I mean by " losing his head; ") what would have happened? Everyone would have gathered round Bateman once more, to support the glorious spirit of blunder. They would have all stood by him and his dull notions, with staunch and splendid obstinacy, and he would probably have produced *The Flowers of the Forest* preceded by *The King and the Miller,* with Irving as the third courtier to the King. A dismal failure would have been the result; Irving would have shaken hands with Bateman; they would have separated; and again, nothing would have come of nothing. Instead of which, the fantastic thing, the thing which no one — or only one — believed in, the thing which the astute manager who was losing money was utterly against, succeeded, and succeeded like wild-fire.

But before coming to the play, of which I have a few reminiscences, I cannot say good-bye to old Bateman as though he did not matter at all; to me he, and the thing he did, matter immensely; there are few things American impresarios have done which matter more. I could sooner spare all the great books on Augustin Daly and other excellent American managers than I can spare the little volume which has yet to be written about splendid old Bateman. *The Innocence of Colonel Bateman* might be the title of the book.

The interesting old fellow who is so set against the production of *The Bells,* is still keen enough to slip over to Paris, where the French version was being given, " to see if he could gain any valuable hints for the English production."

While Brodribb was rehearsing it, a play by C. F. Burnand, based on the same story, and called *Paul Zegers, or the Dream of Retribution,* was produced at the Royal Alfred Theatre, once the Marylebone, where the part of *Mathias,* the Burgomaster, was played by an actor whose name is now unknown — except, in all probability to Mrs. Enthoven. It was produced at that theatre on November 13th, and was a failure. Then, twelve nights later, young Brodribb appeared — shook life out of *The Bells* — and on that night of November 25th, and not before, the greatest actor of the century sprang into existence — Brodribb became Henry Irving.

THE LYCEUM THEATRE

AND NOW we come to that night on which London was given his masterpiece — *The Bells*.

I was not present at the first performance, in 1871, for I was not born, but I think I have seen Irving in it more than thirty times between the years 1889 and 1900, although I never played in the piece. The pieces I never played in under his management, I never watched at rehearsal — to watch a play being rehearsed is in the nature of an intrusion — a kind of eavesdropping — unless you are taking part in the work. I had ample opportunity of seeing many rehearsals of *The Bells* while I was a minor actor in Irving's company, but I never saw one. My old friend, Martin Harvey, the best actor that the company ever produced, could write an interesting essay upon these rehearsals, which I for one would read with delight; for he played in *The Bells,* though he was not in the first production of 1871, being then only four years old.

Gentle reader, you who have seen Irving in this play, you will know that I do not write about him for you; for you saw — you heard — what then do you need more? But some of the others did not see Irving. How shall we together explain him to them?

We who never saw Edmund Kean have a few pictures that speak vividly to us of him, and a few fragments in writing, notably those by Heine and Lord Byron, and we are not skeptical; but today, it is as likely as not that when we speak of Irving we are merely tolerated, for interest in the dramatic craft is not as vivid as it was. You may find a young man or a young woman of today keen to know what it actually was that Irving did, or how he did it, but you will not find many. In fact, like one of those Two Black Crows, they'd " rather hear no more about it."

And here I am, continuing to bore them to death about this event which astonished you and me until 1905 — the year of Irving's death.

How shall I explain this event? There are actors living today, held as great actors by this generation: Irving was not exactly anything like these. We know that — but there is a great singer whom presumably you, the younger generation, do appreciate, and place even higher than the fine actors I have referred to but not mentioned — Chaliapine by name.

When you saw Chaliapine, what did you feel? What do you recall about him? He was pretty good, was he not? I think that you will say that he was really something worth while. There was nothing you could possibly call *charming* about Chaliapine — he was better than that. Speaking of him, you'd never find yourselves saying he was " interesting " or " able " or " intelligent." You would go much further than that. I think you would call him " immense," " magnetic." Well, Irving was all this about twice told. He was twofold what Chaliapine is, because there was greater depth — even as Shakespeare

is greater than Marlowe for all his mighty line, because
of a deep and human beauty which he lets you see.

Have you then caught some faint notion of the idea
"Irving" at last?

And upon Saturday, the 25th of November, 1871 (Bram
Stoker, his biographer, dates this first run as in 1872–73),
the curtain rose at a quarter to eight, and disclosed an
interior scene of a brownish tone . . . a parlour in Alsace.

It is evening. It is snowing outside, and the Burgomaster is expected back at any minute — Irving is expected to appear at any minute. Meantime, the actors
who fill in the preliminary fifteen minutes are filling them
in in a mighty able manner.

These first minutes never failed to charm me. I think
that never was our company seen to better advantage than
during this brief quarter of an hour; and although they
played the whole piece admirably, it was before Irving's
coming onto the stage that they were best.

On his appearance, they one and all fell back into their
places, since to obtrude would have been out of the question. *Ensemble* was achieved, but there was something
to achieve it for, something to which it could lend support; *ensemble* supporting itself, is it not rather a ridiculous spectacle? That's democratic acting if you like —
"for we are jolly good fellows . . . which none of us
will deny."

I am not going to attempt to describe Irving's performance in *The Bells,* or *The Polish Jew,* as it is sometimes called. Stanislavsky, the great Russian theatre
director, has in his memoirs devoted eight pages to a

description of a performance which he seems to say he imagined, or a performance given by the Society of Art and Literature, of which he was a member. I cannot make out from his book which it was — imagined or actually done — and as he omits to date the performance (or the imaginings), though I believe it was in 1891 — twenty years after Irving's — we are unable to know whether these imaginings are original, or are arrived at through suggestions, awakened by hearing someone describe what Irving was like in 1871. He does actually mention Irving by name at the end of the story, but he does it in this way: "*I thought I must have played well, and that I was a tragedian, for the rôle was in the repertoire of such great tragedians as Irving, Barnay, Paul Mounet, and others . . .*" which simply will not do. Stanislavsky has professed all his life *to hate the theatrical in the theatre.* I have heard him say how much he hated it. Well, I believe that an example of the worst part of the "theatrical" is to be found in those six words: "*Irving, Barnay, Paul Mounet, and others.*" For even as *La Tosca* will always belong to Bernhardt, *Othello* to Salvini, and *The Miracle* to Reinhardt, so there was only one great actor who interpreted *The Bells,* and to whom it certainly belongs, and that was Irving. If a second actor of the rôle needs to be mentioned . . . it can only be Coquelin; but to refer to Mounet and Barnay is obviously to be caught in the act of drawing a herring rather theatrically across the trail. Yes, it is one of the worst examples of the theatrical (in that word's worst sense) that I know.

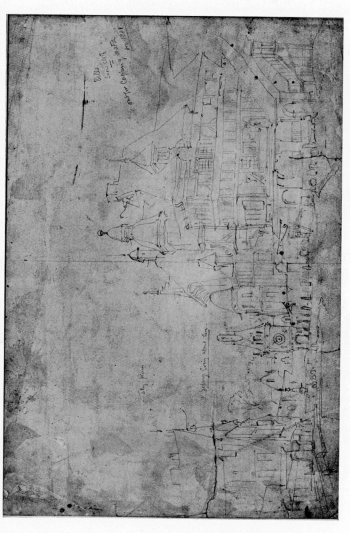

Sketch design for back cloth for "The Bells" — Lyceum Theatre, 1871. Used in Act II, and seen through the windows. It appears to have been used later in "Captain of the Watch," 1881, but what then took place in "The Bells," is not stated. This design is preserved in the Victoria and Albert Museum, London, to which it was presented by R. C. McCleery in 1924.

Since I have referred to this book by Stanislavsky, I may add that it is full of such examples of this particular form of "theatricalism." For professionals I need not explain further, but to others it is perhaps helpful, if I say that it is a state of mind not utterly separate from the Jesuitical state of mind . . . able to give a subtle representation of anything, it can sometimes give an even more subtle misrepresentation.

That theatrical side, I am sure, Stanislavsky despises in himself — for everyone who knows the man is aware of the nobility in his nature and that he is capable of much generosity, except when bitten by that asp, "the theatrical." Amateurs when bitten often suffer — a professional seems to be inoculated from birth. I have stopped to refer to this, for some day the historian will be puzzled that Stanislavsky should seem so innocent of the immensity of our English actor. Let the historian cease from puzzlement, and know that Stanislavsky was a very good actor, and here he was acting.

I HAVE said that I cannot describe Irving's performance in *The Bells:* but though I cannot describe it (and the whole play was merely a series of variations on one theme — Irving), I will try and put down a few notes of little moments remembered.

At his entrance, the applause was so instantaneous that it became part and parcel of the play — without it, or had it been at all lacking in warmth, one could have grown hypercritical, and delivered oneself of some wise words regarding the evil tendency of applause in a playhouse.

In the Moscow Art Theatre in 1909, applause was nearly always prevented. It was held by Stanislavsky to be something offensive — inartistic — and in no way necessary to theatrical performance. I am entirely in accord with this opinion — it is a good rule, "no applause." Irving is the exception here. In *The Bells,* the hurricane of applause at Irving's entrance was no interruption. It was no boisterous greeting by an excitable race, for a blustering actor — it was something which can only be described as part and parcel of the whole, as right as rain. It was a torrent while it lasted. Power responded to power. This applause was no false note, whereas silence would have been utterly false . . . for though Irving endured and did not accept the applause, he deliberately called it out of the spectators. It was necessary *to them* — not to him: it was something they had to experience, or to be rid of, or rather, released from, before they could exactly take in what he was going to give them.

So then, the applause came down like thunder, as Irving appeared in the door-way with the ordinary cry: "It is I." Now no one has ever been known to hear these words distinctly — they resolved themselves into a single exclamation — the door flung open — the figure is in the room, God knows how — with arms extended, face alight, and this single ejaculation: "'t'sI."

In those days — as in the noble days of the Greek Drama — as in those of the Nō Drama of Japan — an important entrance was to be preceded by suspense, and then to come as a surprise, or like a chapter-heading of some grand old romance: it thrilled, and was intended to thrill.

Do you remember these chapter-headings: *The Shoulder of Athos, The Baldric of Porthos,* and *The Handkerchief of Aramis; A Mousetrap in the Seventeenth Century; On the Utility of Stove Pipes:* they come from a book I need not name—and, *How to get rid of Dormice; The Cemetery of the Château d'If:* do you remember the excitement?   Well then—we had reached this state of excitement, of expectancy, of watching, by the time the storm of applause greeted a spectacular entrance on to the stage in these older days.

I can only speak of Irving's entrances, but I believe that with Edmund Kean an entrance was also something to experience.

The *manner of coming on* made it extraordinary with great actors—it was this manner of timing the appearance—measuring its speed and direction—which created a rhythm that was irresistible.

An exit was important too—very important: but the going off of an actor was nothing comparable with the prime importance of his coming on.

To prepare for this entrance in *The Bells,* the entire first fifteen minutes of the play conspired.

The talk all hovered around the thought of the man who was coming, and about other things somehow connected with him.

The storm raging outside the house, the sudden blowing open of a window in the next room, which smashed a whole trayful of crockery and glass as it swung open

— the looking at the clock which told of the overdue trav-
eller — the slow, quiet talk which mumbled on — and
above all, the queer "hurry music," as it is called, which
was astonishingly dramatic: all these things led up to the
first point to be made, and made with decision: "Here is
the man!" And now watch what he will do — better
still, how he will do it — best of all, watch his face and
figure, and follow what it is these are hinting at.

Irving once on, the shout of applause going up, he
lowers his arms, he lowers his head, he relaxes his force
all over, seems to turn it off to an almost dead calm, while
the applause rolls on and up. Twice, maybe three times,
he, as it were, shifts one foot (his right, I think it was),
and by this slight and meaningless gesture a limit is being
reckoned to the applause which goes on and on — no
other motion except that the foot, in shifting, sends a
slight vibration, also without significance, through the
whole person before us — and then as the applause dies
away, at the first sign of it dying, the actor clips it off
by a sudden gesture of awakening from his long and
patiently-endured ordeal — flings cap and whip to right
and left, and begins to shed his coat, his muffler, as his
wife and daughter run to help him off with them.

The story of *The Bells* is this: A man, not by habit or
by instinct a murderer, murders a Polish Jew for his
money. He needs money — his child is crying in its
cradle for food, and by chance this Jew stops at his hut
in a storm, and the man sees him undo a belt which, as it
clanks on the table, emits the sound of untold riches.
This tempts him, he resolves on the deed, and when

the Jew, refreshed by his punch and comforted by the warmth, goes on his way through the snow-storm, the man, taking a short cut across the fields, arrives at a cross-road and, hacking him down with an axe, takes the belt full of gold, drags the body to a limekiln, burns it and, now become rich, relieves the want of his household and thereafter lives a blameless life — finally becoming Burgomaster of his village.

But wherever he goes — whoever speaks to him — whatever he sees or hears, even as he stands speaking to someone about ordinary things, there comes to his ears the far-off sound of the sledge-bells of the Polish Jew. Haunted by this, he lives his life in sorrow which increases and increases until one night, dreaming that he is in the dock and being convicted and sentenced to death, he wakes only to die, believing that he is being hanged.

The thing Irving set out to do was to show us the sorrow which slowly and remorselessly beat him down. As, no matter who the human being may be, and what his crime, the sorrow which he suffers must appeal to our hearts, so Irving set out to wring our hearts, not to give us a clever exhibition of antics such as a murderer would be likely to go through. He does not appeal to any silly sentimentality in you — he merely states the case by showing you that quite obviously here is a strong human being who, through a moment of weakness, falls into error and becomes for two hours a criminal — does what he knows he is doing — acts deliberately — but (and here is Irving) acts automatically, as though impelled by an immense force, against which no resistance is possible.

To return to the moment after the first entrance — the process of getting rid of his coat and brushing off the snow as he stands on the mat by the door being over, he works his way down to a chair in the centre (Irving was always in the centre — he had no inferiority complex) and there, taking off his boots, he begins to put on and buckle his shoes.

Now you might think that the act of taking off some boots could be done in one way only — but the way Irving did it had never been thought of till he did it, and has never been done since.

It was, in every gesture, every half move, in the play of his shoulders, legs, head and arms, mesmeric in the highest degree — slowly we were drawn to watch every inch of his work as we are drawn to read and linger on every syllable of a strangely fine writer.

It was the perfection of craftsmanship.

While he is taking off the boots and pulling on the shoes, the men at the table, who are smoking and drinking lazily, are telling in drawling tones that just before he came in, they were saying that they did not remember a night like this since what was called the Polish Jew's winter.

By the time the speaker had got this slowly out — and it was dragged purposely — Irving was buckling his second shoe, seated, and leaning over it, with his two long hands stretched down over the buckles. We suddenly saw these fingers stop their work; the crown of the head suddenly seemed to glitter and become frozen — and then, at the pace of the slowest and most terrified snail, the two hands, still motionless and dead, were seen to be coming up the side of the leg . . . the whole torso of the man, also seeming frozen, was gradually, and by an almost imperceptible movement, seen to be drawing up and back, as it would straighten a little, and to lean a little against the back of the chair on which he was seated.

Once in that position — motionless — eyes fixed ahead of him and fixed on us all — there he sat for the space of ten to twelve seconds, which, I can assure you, seemed to us all like a lifetime, and then said — and said in a voice deep and overwhelmingly beautiful: " Oh, you were talking of that — were you? " And as the last syllable was uttered, there came, afar off, the regular throbbing sound of sledge-bells.

There he sat looking at us, and there sat the others, smoking and musing and comfortably motionless, except for the smoke from their pipes — and on and on went the sound of these bells — on and on and on — nothing else. Again, I assure you that time seemed out of joint, and moved as it moves to us who suffer, when we wish it would move on and it does not stir.

And the next step of his dance began.

He moves his head slowly from us — the eyes still somehow with us — and moves it to the right — taking as long as a long journey to discover a truth takes. He looks to the faces on the right — nothing: slowly the head revolves back again, down, and along the tunnels of thought and sorrow, and at the end the face and eyes are bent upon those to the left of him . . . utter stillness

. . . nothing there either — everyone is concerned with his or her little doings — smoking or knitting or unravelling wool or scraping a plate slowly and silently — a long pause, endless, breaking our hearts, comes down over everything, and on and on go these bells. Puzzled, motionless . . . he glides up to a standing position: never has anyone seen another rising figure which slid slowly up like that: with one arm slightly raised, with sensitive hand speaking of far-off apprehended sounds, he asks, in the voice of some woman who is frightened, yet does not wish to frighten those with her: " Don't you . . . don't you hear the sound of sledge-bells on the road? " " Sledge-bells? " grumbles the smoking man; " Sledge-bells? " pipes his companion; " Sledge-bells? " says the wife — all of them seemingly too sleepy and comfortable to apprehend anything . . . see anything . . . or understand . . . and, as they grumble a negative, suddenly he staggers, and shivers from his toes to his neck; his jaws begin to chatter; the hair on his forehead, falling over a little, writhes as though it were a nest of little snakes. Everyone is on his feet at once, to help: " Caught a chill " . . . " Let's get him to bed " . . . and *one* of the moments of the immense and touching dance closes — only one — and the next one begins, and the next after — figure after figure of exquisite pattern and purpose is unfolded, and then closed, and ever a new one unfolded in its wake.

I can write no more; you may perhaps have felt something . . . I don't know — but, if you did, I know it was one thousandth part of what we felt. As we watched this figure, we felt as silent and as still as when we hear of things too sad to realize; and when it was over and we might move, we knew that this was the finest point that the craft of acting could reach.[1]

[1] You will say, perhaps, that Irving seems to have explained so much to us that the other characters in the play were daft not to notice too; that a hundred times, by eavesdropping, they might have caught him giving us a full explanation that he was the culprit.

You are quite right. Irving followed the most ancient and unshakable tradition, which says that the Dramatist is to take his audience into his confidence. The actor who fails to observe this fails as an actor. I have seen such actors recently in London. The villain of the play comes on the stage smiling: he is quite alone; and though he remains alone for five minutes, he does not dare to tell us that he is " the villain " — has not dared to let any tell-tale look escape him, and he fails to explain anything to us. It is called realism — it is no such thing: it is merely incompetence — an incapacity to understand that *everything* has to be clearly explained to the spectators, and little or no thought paid to whether the other characters on the stage overhear or see. If they overhear, if they see, they too have failed in the simplest rudiments of their craft.

THE ACTOR

HIS VOICE

IT WAS brought against Irving that he could not speak our English tongue. This accusation went on for some twenty years or so, after which folk gave it up, despairing of teaching Irving how English should be spoken.

Irving, never deaf to criticism, tried to speak as neatly, as nicely as any sucking dove; but, when he grew a little excited, as is customary with great actors, he would return to his old way of utterance.

He would say "*Gud*" for "*God*"; "*Cut thrut dug*" for "*Cut throat dog*" (*Shylock*); "*Tack the rup frum mey nek*" for "*Take the rope from my neck*" (*Mathias in The Bells*); "*Ritz*" for "*Rich*" (*Mathias*); this word *rich*, spoken as *ritz — ritz — ritz — ritz,* he repeated, as some will remember, during the scene of dreaming, where he imagines he is in a field and awaiting the coming of the Polish Jew, and hears the bells of his sledge afar off, coming nearer and nearer. The effect of the *ritz* instead of *rich* was this: instead of the sound reminding us of an old housewife shooing the fowls away from the kitchen door, we were horribly thrilled, as at the ominous sound of the serpent about to strike, and we were aware that a duet between the regular throb of the bells and this voice was being sung. At the end of a long sustained series of these sounds, he sprang — he struck down the imaginary Jew — and fell in a heap on top of him.

Again, when, in the same dream, he spoke the line:
" *How the dogs howl at Daniel's farm — how they how
-ow-owl-l-l,*" it had to be admitted that we never said it
like that — I must confess that it can be only once said
so, and by one man only, and in this very scene. But
how it stirred the imagination, this one word.

Yet again, in *Macbeth,* the passage " *To trammel up
the consequence,*" became in his mouth, " *tram-mele
up-p the cunsequnce* " — a sharp division of the two m's,
a brief stop after the first, second, and the fourth words.

To our English ears, other English speakers were less
curious; easier with these speakers it was " *do drammel ub
ze gonsequence,*" or " *to tramluptheconsquence* " — and
if this last was a simple way out of the difficulty, it will be
admitted that, after all, it is a difficult word to hear, to
believe in, and to remember, if easy enough to swallow.

For *good,* Irving said *god — sight* was *seyt — stood* was
stod — smote became *smot — hand* was often *hond* or
hend.

In short, his tendency was to enrich the sounds of
words — to make them expressive, rather than what the
unskilful in England take to be refined.

And I was far away from Irving one day in 1919, when
I rode from Sabbioneta to Casalmaggiore, and as I rode
began to read a sixteenth-century ballad of *Robin and the
Potter.* The good old English song begins like this:

> In schomer, when the levès spryng,
> The bloschems on every bowe,
> So merey doyt the berdỳs synge
> Yn wodỳs merey now.

It is not too easy to read difficult stuff like this, in small type, as you ride in an old four-wheeled rackety *carrozza* on the billowy side-road leading out of Sabbioneta. So I took the ballad slowly, line by line, pronouncing each word aloud to myself, so that the sounds would strike familiarly on my ear, in tune and time, and make good to the hearing what was strange to the eyes.

I had not read more than four to five verses when I felt I was in Nottinghamshire; it was summer, green willows and aspens on each side, birds sang in the woods — it was pleasant. I went on until something like the fourteenth verse, when I was up to an old trick again; my pencil was marking the book, and down in the margin went the two initials, *H. I.,* not once, but five or six times. But I went on quickly, and forgot *H. I.* for Robin Hood.

Opening this book some seven or eight years later, I see these pencil marks, and I think I will copy out the verses around which, for some evident purpose, they flutter as though some little nest were hidden there.

These are two of the verses beside which I find my pencilled *H. I.'s:*

> Togeder then went *thes* two *yemen,*
> Het was a *god seyt* to *se;*
> Therof low Robyn h*es* men,
> Ther they st*od od*onder a *tre.*
>
> Leytell John to hes felowhes seyde,
> *Yend* potter [1] *welle* steffeley stonde.
> The potter, with a caward stroke,
> Sm*ot* [2] the bokeler owt of h*es* honde.[3]

[1] Irving would have said "p*u*t-ter."
[2] "Smot," to rhyme with "hot" — not "smote" with "boat."
[3] The italics are mine.

Then come several more *H. I.'s,* against such lines as: " Hes bokeler at hes *fette* " — what *we* call " his *feeeet,*" but which is here pronounced *fette,* like *wet-t;* and " I *well prey* the god potter," and " What ys *they* name? seyde the potter." On reading the whole ballad again, this time indoors, I am no longer in Nottinghamshire, I am at the Lyceum Theatre, and I become very aware of Irving, and I hear again as it were the old voice; and as I listen to this pure old English strain, I think how strange it is that it is always for preserving the best that men lay themselves open to the attacks of their fellows.

For this is the old English speech, and Irving brought back to us something of the ripe old sounds, and dammé if we didn't object.

Some fifty years before Irving's time, 2,000,000 English schoolboys were being taught by some 8000 English schoolmistresses and ushers to say "God," and mean the Almighty: the " o " was insisted on; it was to sound noble — i.e., frozen: it was to sound like the word " gourd." " Once again, Billy. 'Gourd.' No, Billy, 'Gourd'" . . . Billy tries, and then says "Guud ". . . " Now, Billy, I give you two more chances before I use my prerogative." Billy, trembling before the whistling shadow of the prerogative, drops one " u " the more — then another, and, in a burst of religious fervour, and dashing for the " ur," comes out with " Gorrd," and the deadly and the hard once more triumph over the real and the beautiful.

And so by Irving's time all " o's " were hard and deadly, all " e's " were brayed or mewed, all double " oo's " became " u's," and " a's " were flattened; all kinds of contortions were employed to bring out the full horror of the nobility of each vowel and the sweetness of each consonant, and now on the day of victory, the nation hugs to its breast its immense defects.

It comes to it that it was because Irving's calling permitted, even expected, him to boil when about to speak, that, availing himself of this permission and doing as he was expected, he came to speak English as I believe it should be spoken, and as this same good rich English was always spoken in the days of Robin Hood, and long before and after.

It was an unfortunate thing for Irving and his critics; for while they both agreed, theoretically, that " o " should be pronounced like " o," and not like " u," Irving fell from grace every time he got near an " o," and uttered it like a " u "; and his critics, while theoretically quite in sympathy with him, had, in presence of an enlightened public, to rap him sharply over the knuckles for what they considered sheer carelessness. "Do I say ' Gud ' when I say ' Gud ' ? " asked Irving, and it had to be admitted, with an apologetic cough, that he *did,* though some had the grace to add: " but yer Inglish is perfict, moy dear fellar."

And so, while Irving's was " perfict Inglish," it was none the less asseverated that he could not speak our mother tongue — and even that his amazing range of sound was monotonous!

Ever since I can remember, theorists have said that Irving mutilated the rhythm whenever he came to speak verse. When asked how Irving might have improved, these theorists would either begin to caterwaul unctuously

— which may, for all I know, have been rhythmic, but was ridiculous — or they would mutter as paterfamilias does at evening prayers, and there seemed to be no health in them. In short, they were unable to utter six words beautifully, yet would be instructing one of the best verse speakers of the age.

I see that the brilliant translator of Greek plays, Professor Gilbert Murray, has recently returned to the attack. After referring to the " Mad bull " period of declaiming verse (the Barry Sullivan way of dealing with it), he writes: *" Then came a style for which Henry Irving must bear some responsibility, a style in which, in order to escape from the smooth monotony of verse rhythm, the actor deliberately mutilated and wrecked the rhythm, and tried to turn the verse into prose."*

Irving need bear no " responsibility " whatever, since he never " deliberately mutilated or wrecked the rhythm."

And suppose for a moment that he had done so — even as Professor Murray is supposed to have deliberately distorted the rhythm and sense of the Greek plays, in his enchanting translations — then we have only to remind ourselves that there are some people (a very few) who are justified in doing what others are not justified in doing. *Charles Surface* tipsy is not at all the same thing as *Bill Sykes* drunk. Anyhow, I am eager to hear Professor Murray declaiming Shakespearean verse: very.

" Next to the faculty of discernment, diamonds and pearls are the rarest things in the world," says La Bruyère — and indeed, if something rare be worth the having, it is well to wait a long time before asserting that an

Irving cannot speak English, a Shakespeare cannot write plays, a Rossini cannot compose an opera and a Blake cannot draw. Yet this is what we hear, and have heard continually, year in and year out — Byron is no poet, Mozart no musician, and Mussolini cannot rule.

To sum up, Irving was a great actor, speaking perfectly, moving faultlessly, amongst people who for the most part spoke sloppily and moved without grace.

This is what my mother writes in her memoirs:

Once when I was touring with him in America, at the time when he was at the highest point of his fame, I watched him one day in the train — always a delightful occupation, for his face provided many pictures a minute — and being struck by a curious look, half puzzled, half despairing, asked him what he was thinking about.

" I was thinking," he answered slowly, " how strange it is that I should have made the reputation I have as an actor, with nothing to help me — with no equipment. My legs, my voice — everything has been against me. For an actor who can't walk, can't talk, and has no face to speak of, I've done pretty well."

THE ACTOR

HIS MOVEMENT AND HIS FACE

As he jerks along the street with league-devouring stride, his long, dark hair hanging over his shoulders, his look dreamy and absent, his cheeks wan and thin, the slovenly air with which his clothes are worn, people turn to stare after him. . .
— The World, 1877.[1]

SOME day the historian of the Theatre, searching for information about Irving, may chance to light upon a little book by Mr. William Archer, written in 1883, entitled *Henry Irving, Artist and Manager: A Critical Study.* He is to take it from me that much that the good Archer wrote of Irving in this booklet is not true. Intending to be utterly fair, if critical, scholarly but just, the well-intentioned author simply fails to be either just or fair.

For example, he says that Irving murdered our mother tongue; to state it more simply, that he could not speak the King's English — which is untrue. And *" What shall I say of his walk? . . . How describe it? "* he asks, adding, *" it is as difficult to describe as it is easy to imitate,"* which also is untrue: he says further that Irving, like the marionette, loses command of his legs, and that he depresses the head, protrudes the shoulders, that his locomo-

---

[1] This extract from *The World* of 1877, edited by Mr. Edmund Yates, was reprinted in Mr. Brereton's *Life of Henry Irving.* I came across a copy in which someone had pencilled against the words *" the slovenly air with which his clothes are worn," " Excuse me! He was always very well dressed. W. D."* I believe the initials stand for Walter Dowdeswell.

tion is the result of an involuntary spasm, accompanied by extraordinary sidelong and backward skirmishings, reminding one of the movements of a napkin-ring when suddenly shot from under the forefinger. But he adds: "*his motions can be, and often are, those of a normal human being.*"

Had he asked me what he should say of Irving's walk, and "how describe it," I should have said: "My dear Archer, describe it, if you must speak of it at all, as a whole language!" I should have been obliged to add: "If you know what I mean," for Mr. Archer was slow in the uptake in these matters. But I am glad I had never read this book by William Archer until today. . . Today it comes freshly, and proves so useful.

No; the good William Archer would not have understood what it was I meant by saying that Irving's walk was a whole language. He understood nothing about Irving, and passed along this misunderstanding to his friend, Mr. Bernard Shaw. But Archer always tried to speak the truth.

Archer — being a dramatic critic, and one of the foremost of his day — should, one feels, have taken especial pains to understand the great tragedian of the time, not merely because he was great and popular, but for the more interesting reason — that he was a very difficult actor to understand, a very excellent actor to interpret with care, so as to leave behind a record of him by which all future English actors might learn how to act. This, with more understanding, Archer might have done, and failed to do.

It was not so difficult to appreciate Irving in the broad way the public did, but to follow him curiously and to delight in his technique needed an understanding of the dramatic art as it has been taught and practised for centuries all the world over. It was in this understanding that William Archer was deficient.

Irving can be said to have been essentially a traditional actor. Although he broke with a number of ridiculous English conventions, decayed traditions that were obviously not worth preserving, or traditions that did not suit his purpose, he never broke with any of the nobler ancient traditions: in fact he preserved them sacredly, so that a critic like William Archer, who was no dash-ahead young fellow, who was destined to make no splash in the world, to dazzle the minds of none of his readers, but was a good, jog-trot, honest, proper young man — such a lad, on becoming a dramatic critic, might have been most careful to study and to understand this actor, who, though rooted in tradition, had a voice of his own, movements of his own, and some ideas of his own . . . this actor who was to prove to be the greatest England has ever given birth to.

We have discovered that he could speak, let us now see whether he could walk. Archer was not the only critic who mumbled that "the man can't walk."

Now how odd this is, for I never yet heard any one of the thousand people who passed him in the street assert that he was flying, skating, or paddling along. And I think that there is no one who saw him in a street or a room, in private life, who denied that he walked perfectly, or who failed to observe that no one could walk incomparably as he. There was, of course, the usual " paid assassin," the *Disinterested Observer* — the jolly old hireling of the Press, who earned a fairly good salary by what Irving's biographer calls " scurrilous attacks," and there was the caricaturist who, not over-observant himself, preferred to rely upon *Disinterested Observer* for his pictures — drawing what he described. I never thought " Ape " so poor as when, on December 19, 1874, he gave us *The Bells* in that week's *Vanity Fair*. Better by far were A. B.'s caricatures, and best of all, though less comic, Sargent's one parody. All the caricaturists attributed to Irving bent knees, bent back, or a dragging leg — like the æsthete in *Iolanthe* — which, if not particularly funny, was anyhow quite untrue.

For no one walked so well. Actors as a rule walk with precision and grace, and all who saw him will tell you that Irving walked perfectly naturally — but only in private life. As he stepped upon the boards of his theatre, at rehearsal, something was added to the walk — a consciousness. And this was right. He became aware of the boards — the ordinary life was being put away — something was coming into his blood — he could not feel the same as when on the paving stones of Bond Street. While we gathered together on the stage at nine o'clock, rolling onto it somewhat ponderously, as befits good hefty assistants, suddenly comes Irving with a spring in his heels. It was really quite interesting to those of us who loved to watch him, to observe this difference — it meant mischief.

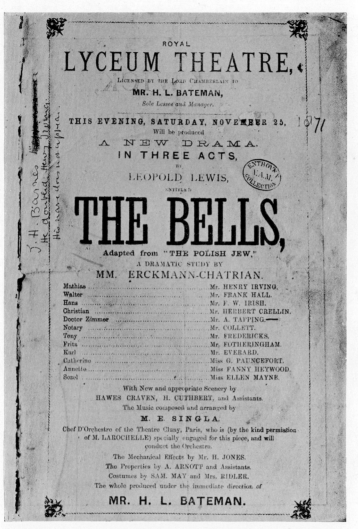

Programme of first night of "The Bells" at the Lyceum Theatre, London, 1871. *By courtesy of the Victoria and Albert Museum.*

But if, to Irving's ordinary walk in daily life, a springing motion was added at rehearsal, it was only a forecast of what was to come at night.

At night, Archer, who, excluded from rehearsals, was then allowed to come into the theatre for a couple of hours, provided he sat down in a seat on the other side of the footlights, Archer is wringing his hands and crying: "What can I say of his walk? It isn't walking!"

My dear old Archer, you were right for once. It wasn't walking. It was dancing!

In dancing his rôle, Irving went to the extreme limits possible to an actor of the nineteenth century, of preserving the last tingle of the mighty Greek tradition. He was not ill informed about that tradition, but he held and expressed a few ill-considered opinions about it. He wrote rather freezingly about "tragedy on stilts," and the artificiality of Greek theatre work. Yet of all the actors of the nineteenth century, he instinctively expressed in his work his devotion to the Greek idea — for in his bones he felt its ancient fires revive.

He danced, he did not merely walk — he sang, he by no means merely spoke. He was essentially artificial in distinction to being merely natural. It was all this which puzzled the earnest normality of William Archer and a dozen more ingenuous critics of those days.[2] It was all this which carried the rest of us off our feet — a song and a dance generally do.

---

[2] If I have shown little sympathy for Archer, it is mainly because he was so unsympathetic towards Irving. This fact cannot in the least detract from my admiration for his work as a critical student of acting. For his valuable study, *Masks or Faces* (1888) I have a particular regard.

I am told that the great French actor of that day, Mounet-Sully, understood what it was to sing and dance a rôle. I never saw him, so I cannot say. The cleverest French actor of the day, Coquelin, was a very fine comedian — one of the finest — essentially a fine matter-of-fact comedian, as compared with Irving or Mounet-Sully. In his voice you might detect little trills and the sound of instruments, but for all this he kept his feet from pirouetting and twinkling, and was looked on as essentially a reasonable actor. Wisely he interpreted the wisest of plays — the plays of Molière — for happily he had been trained in his very house — the Comédie Française.

With Irving it was quite different. Shakespeare had no house — no home — he and all of us were wandering vagabonds, and we are wanderers still. The mere erection of a National Theatre or of a Memorial Theatre at Stratford, though it may please some if only on account of the large outlay in stone and machinery, cannot give us a home, for a home is not a house created by any material: it is what you who have made one, know it to be. No place like it, you say: and you are right, when good spirits make a home. The spirit of intrigue never yet made one, and it is intrigue, not straightforwardness, which has laboured towards the erection of the Stratford Memorial Theatre and the National Theatre. It is best that someone shall state this, when tact has proved powerless to prevent such big blunders.

Not having a home in which to train himself, Irving did as many other great actors of England have done — he took Shakespeare as his guide and master. Little, but successful actors prefer to take up with the latest thing — not so Irving. And Shakespeare helped him, for in Shakespeare is a great, a curious rhythm, and it was this he captured. In what an audacious manner does Shakespeare break the staid laws which the steadier poets preserve as they would preserve their lives! How he risks all, and with all the ease of an adventurer. When in that mood, he cannot slip — and all his errors, great or small, serve but to make him who he is — Shakespeare, and not, positively not, one of the Elizabethans. Is Irving not to do this too, if he can? Indeed he does it — he did it, and became Irving, not merely a Victorian. Endless seemed the labour to achieve this — no school to help. So Irving trained himself, and began to prance and turn and glide and sing, and — it began to go all right.

Now if William Archer had taken the trouble to read Shakespeare aloud, he would never have failed to understand what it was that Irving was doing. Irving had caught the most difficult Shakespearean rhythm, and was suiting the action to the word.

Every now and again the words were natural, but as a rule they were more than natural — they were highly artificial. And thus it came about that Irving positively designed (as M. Fokine has designed) dances which fitted perfectly to the speeches given him by Shakespeare.

When he came to melodrama, to *The Bells, The Lyons Mail,* or *Louis XI,* he realized that a good deal more dance would be needed to hold up these pieces — and then it was that, putting out all his skill, he wiped the floor with the rôle and danced it like the devil. When it was Shakespeare he was dealing with, he had merely to wipe the beautiful glass window-panes. His movements were all measured. He was forever counting — one, two, three — pause — one, two — a step, another, a halt, a faintest turn, another step, a word. (Call it a beat, a foot, a step, all is one — I like to use the word "step.") That constituted one of his dances. Or seated on a chair, at a table — raising a glass, drinking — and then lowering his hand and glass — one, two, three, four — suspense — a slight step with his eyes — five — then a patter of steps — two slow syllables — another step — two more syllables — and a second passage in his dance was done. And so right through the piece — whatever it might be — there was no chance movement; he left no loose ends. All was sharp cut at beginning and end, and all joined by an immensely subtle rhythm — the Shakespearean rhythm — discerned by Brodribb when wondering how to do it, and not a soul to tell him how.

From the first to the last moment that Irving stood on the stage, each moment was significant . . . every sound, each movement, was intentional — clear-cut, measured dance: nothing real — all massively artificial — yet all flashing with the light and the pulse of nature. A fine style.

His movements being measured, rhythmic, planned, it may be too obvious to state that the action of his face was part of all this, and was measured too: yet it may not have occurred to one or two of my readers that this control of feature till immobility was achieved, constituted a mask.

Some actors paint away one face and make themselves another face; they even build up these faces — one for every new part: but then these actors have little to say with the face. It stands to reason that if you have much to say with the face, the sooner it becomes a mask, the quicker you'll be able to speak with it. For a mask never fidgets; it endures, and at the slightest touch it becomes expressive, it lights up and speaks.

Irving was all for these slight, significant touches. Anything sprawling was simply not Irving. With him all had to be delicate, economical work — all done in sharp-cut lines, no bungling — no rough-and-tumble.

Spontaneity he valued, but seldom indulged in: what he did, he did by design. He did not respect that artlessness which fails to reveal art. He was not merely fond of his art — his art of acting was his religion. To be playful and go-as-you-please about it — to be spontaneous, unless by the grace of God — was to him a sign of idiocy.

There seems to have been a day when, after witnessing what is called "an inspired performance of genius," "full of feeling," he took himself aside and said: "My boy, listen to me. In the next twenty or thirty years, you may be called upon to perform some eight thousand times, and as you may possibly not feel inspired each time you perform, you may, during the course of a very stren-u-ous rôle, not feel inspired for more than — er — let us say — um — ten minutes per act. I think, therefore, you will do well to remember that by taking great pains you can, shall we say — um — *design* a part, a rôle, so carefully that, inspired or not, you'll be demmed interesting. The less 'feeling' the better. See what I mean, my boy?"

And so it was that each syllable and each pause, each step and each look, was as nearly perfectly designed and of a piece with the whole as could possibly be.

I believe that this is what the great actors of Japan did — designed their parts — and I believe they still do it.

Unlike the Japanese actors, Irving was not athletic. He could on occasion bound across the stage, when it was imperative, but he did not seek for opportunities to display the agility that was in his wiry frame; Harlequin had done that for so many years, and done it to perfection. No, the really agile portion of his body was his face — his mask.[3]

The faces of some actors are podgy and loquacious, saying an infinite deal of nothing: his was clean-cut, expressionless till he let it speak, and when it spoke it said one thing at a time, clearly.

"But was he natural?" is always being asked. Indeed he was — natural like lightning — but not natural like the ape. Some there are who will for ever think that to be commonplace is to be natural. They find it very natural in an actor to drift on and off the stage, to tactfully avoid saying or doing anything that might astonish any-

---

[3] I think it was this which went far towards persuading people that Irving was an *intellectual* actor. He never pretended to more intellect than a great actor need possess: a millionaire hardly ever bothers to parade his possessions, and Irving was rich in all that is necessary to an actor — nothing more than that.

one in the audience — to look and act as much like a cypher as possible — slightly sleepy about the eyes — toll-loll. To these, then, it must appear that if an actor is expressive he is unnatural — if he astonishes, he is positively eccentric — if he is dramatic, a scandal.

Irving was astonishing us always — he was terrible in tragedy: not terrifying as a sudden thunder-clap, but as when the whole of nature seems to suffer and to become more still and more and more quiet, so did Irving do. There is a flash — something is struck — something terrible has happened, without rumblings or crash. These come afterwards; then the clouds conspire and, like a crowd of actors, create a fearful noise — but the tragedy, the terrible thing, has happened. The force which struck and blinded us, has withdrawn, and is once again veiled within its secret temple. Irving in tragedy was not like the storm which splutters out, but like one which gathers and then strikes, once. Once aware of this, we were awake.

AGAIN, Irving was natural, yet highly artificial. He was natural in that he did not remind one of either an ape or a god, but of a man. He was artificial, as certain plants seem artificial — we don't call them artificial flowers, for they are actually alive and growing. And Irving was artificial as these — as an orchid — as a cactus — exotic and stately, forbidding, and so curiously composed as to be what we may call architectural — attractive as are all shapely things.

Every moment was formed.

There are plants which lag and straggle, such as *Love lies bleeding:* Irving was not like that.

A short while ago, two of our dramatic critics were differing one with the other about Bravura and Quietism — and in the course of their argument, said many an interesting thing. One of these referred to the skill of Bernhardt and Irving "in the art of overstatement." Duse he cited as "scorning a climax," and as having "stripped utterly away from her art any of the habitual emotional flights and bravura of the playhouse." In another place he refers to Bernhardt's bravura and Duse's quietism. I am not here concerned with either of these fine actresses — only with Irving: and as it may be supposed some day that he was one of these — a bravurista or a quietist — I had better put it on record that he was neither.

What is Quietism, and what Bravura?

Quietism: "a passive attitude towards life, especially as a form of religious mysticism."

Bravura: "brilliant execution, display of exceptional powers; passage requiring this: a musical term."

So we see that the two words cannot possibly be used when comparing the acting of one genius with that of another: for a genius is both a quietist and a bravurista.

But the good intention of the two critics was to make it clear to us that they were talking of two extremes. Let us accept the word Bravura as being a stage term, and let me find another word for Quietism

Bravura comes from the Italian, and means " courage," "bravery ": not a quiet courage, but of the more obvious and dashing order. Clearly it refers to expression, in distinction to something unexpressed.

So that Bravura is a good word to use about the expressive part of stage things — it stands for swagger.

Quietism will not do as a word for our purpose. In place of it, at a pinch, we could substitute Psalmody, which is " mere recitation with a slight inflexion," or briefly, " psalm singing."

If we use the word Bravura, we are bound to use as its antithesis another musical term. So let us say Psalmody.

But what does it all come to in the end — do we not resolve the two words into " passionate " and " passionless " — " personal " and " impersonal " — " cold " and " hot " — we can go on for a very long time. Black and white have ever stood apart, and people have never tired of trying to keep them apart — yet grey exists, spite of that, is necessary, and hurts neither black nor white. Penny plain and twopence coloured is another nice division — we know what it means: some of us put a higher price on the coloured print than on the plain one; some do not. I see reason for accepting both and paying twopence for either — when good. There is something of quietism, the impersonal, the passionless, in the twopence coloured; there is something of bravura in the penny plain.

There is in all good theatre work a measure of each — " *Between two worlds life hovers like a star* " — it is the first line of the ninety-ninth verse of the fifteenth Canto of *Don Juan*.

Irving was skilful neither in understatement nor in overstatement: he stated with precision — neither too much nor too little — he hovered between the two. He was fond of Talma's statement that "tragic acting is the result of the union of grandeur without pomp, and nature without triviality." Masters achieve this, and Irving was a master — " an incomparable actor," wrote Mounet-Sully: and when the great French actor says that, we do well to leave it unquestioned. Yet the odious are for ever comparing him with other actors; with Barry Sullivan, or with Salvini. That Salvini was a superlatively great actor, we have been told by every judge of acting who has ever written of him. Salvini first appeared in London in 1875, at Drury Lane Theatre, at the age of forty-six. He appeared as *Othello*.

Now in London at this time there were two remarkable men, who faced each other every evening in that Theatre Royal, the House of Commons — Disraeli and Gladstone.

I suppose no one ever attempted to compare these two, and it seems hardly probable that anyone will attempt a comparison — any more than one could compare Othello and Iago — or Salvini and Irving.

Gladstone and Salvini roll their words out, they stride, they glare very grandly and are spacious: you want to look and listen to them. Disraeli and Irving do something quite different. They glide, they are terribly self-possessed, their eyes dart flame: you *have* to look and listen to them, whether you want to or no. Rhetoric is for whoever likes to use it — not for Disraeli or Irving. "He will say something fine" is what listeners would murmur to themselves in the presence of Gladstone or of Salvini — and fine it was. But the same listeners, when watching Disraeli or Irving, would not know where they were, who exactly this being in front of them could be, and would think to themselves, "What will he say — what will he do now?"

That is a very vast difference from being sure of what is coming. With Irving, nothing could be calculated on; anything might happen, and at any moment — he never disappointed one there — and the opposite to that which one half expected, generally did happen.

How frail he seemed at times — and how deadly, or how touching, that smile — how deliberate that walk — ever compelling, winning, and technically perfect, so that a beauty hung on all his words and all his movements. Even in crude melodrama his work was exquisite, for it was perfect, and thus made exquisite that crude thing.

The actor and the artist can see this best, and all actors will tell you what I tell you here. The ordinary playgoer can see it too. I have heard Mr. Walter Dowdeswell speak of Irving as though he, Dowdeswell, had been an actor, instead of an expert in pictures — and he would touch on Irving as though he were speaking of the technique of some fine Italian painter. But I have read things by dramatic critics, by Mr. George Bernard Shaw, for example, which prove that Mr. Shaw saw nothing at all — maybe because he was no actor, certainly no artist, and quite unconcerned by the many little things so much loved by the wise.

So THEN, as we cannot compare Gladstone and Disraeli, Irving and Salvini, Duse and Bernhardt, since they are all six of them incomparable, the words Bravura and Quietism, if used at all in discussing the stage, must be reserved for those actors and actresses who form groups — whose work is so much a matter of *ensemble* — who are not outstanding figures. It is, of course, permissible to note marked dissimilarities. For example, the little Kean, the huge Salvini — the versatility of Garrick, with Macklin's predisposition for one kind of rôle. Very marked was Salvini's preference for *Othello,* wherein he shone with such splendour — whereas in *Hamlet,* in *Shylock* (I am told he attempted it) we know he was like nothing at all: in *Romeo,* (had he attempted it), in *Iago,* in *The Bells,* or as *Doricourt,* what would he have been like?

So we may safely say that whereas Garrick, Kean, and Irving were able to act anything, Salvini was strictly limited to a few massive rôles — and in these there was no one to approach him.

Irving could play *Doricourt* on Monday and *Mathias* on Tuesday, on Wednesday *Iago,* and on Thursday *Hamlet;* on Friday *Shylock;* on Saturday afternoon *Malvolio or Wolsey,* and on Saturday evening *Dubosc.* No one can deny that this it is to be able to act.

Add to these very dissimilar rôles those of *Dr. Primrose, Digby Grant, Charles the First, Philip* in *Queen Mary, Richelieu,* and *Corporal Brewster* — each of which was

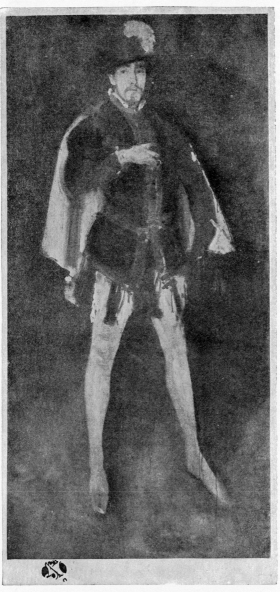

Portrait of Irving as *King Philip,* in Tennyson's *Queen Mary*
(1876), painted by James McNeill Whistler. Reproduced from
a rare photograph, signed by Whistler, and in the possession of
the author. The picture is here shown in an earlier state than
when it passed into Irving's hands, and as a portrait it is far
more like him than the later version (reproduced in the books
of Ellen Terry and Bram Stoker, and in Irving's *The Drama*).
The doublet worn by Irving in 1876, and shown here, was
worn in 1892 by the author of this book, when he played the
part of *Cromwell* in *Henry VIII* at the Lyceum Theatre.

perfect in its way, and no mere sketch — and I think you will not find another actor of such calibre, possessed of such astounding versatility.

He was, people will tell you, " always Irving," and this is said for a very interesting and sound reason — because people have nothing else to say.

IRVING AS STAGE-MANAGER

I HAD almost headed this chapter *Irving as Producer,* but strictly speaking, Irving was not a producer: I am forced again into a repetition — he was an actor — an actor manager. He set out, not to produce a play as we do today — as they did in Italy in the seventeenth and eighteenth centuries — but to act one: he stage-managed it himself, but he stage-managed for one actor's sake, for the sake of Irving — and a producer does not do that.

Irving was an actor, and an actor only — all he did and all he thought, rightly or wrongly, was imagined or done as an actor.

I want to make this point. It is the only point I wish you to allow me to insist on. He felt things, thought things, saw things, heard things, and did things as an actor should — not as every actor does, but as a unique one can do. He was this unique actor.

Maybe you begin to suspect that Irving was what today we call precious. Yes, he was that, too . . . very precious — as diamonds would like to be once more. Now comes the dread upon you that Irving was deuced highbrow stuff — you've hit it; very highbrow stuff — as high as Olympus, if you follow me.

This extra-ordinary actor engaged himself as his ordinary stage-manager. The title "stage-manager" is more ancient than that of "producer" and, I always think, more honourable too — which is my reason for using it here. Maybe the producer of today has to take more responsibility than the stage-manager of old times. A producer has to think of everything, so he will think of everyone, but he will not think of himself, as he is not to appear on the stage during the performance. He is supposed to be able to visualize the whole thing better than a stage-manager was wont to do, and he is supposed to be less theatrical, and more of an artist; to depend less upon getting his results through theatrical dodges — in short, he is supposed to be a far more virtuous fellow than was the old stage-manager. But even if he be less rough, I do not think he is any readier. He certainly has more time in which to study — has he more common sense or better taste? All depends on whom you select as your idea of a first-class producer — Piscator, the late Sir Augustus Harris, or Smythe. Piscator is a young man of ideas, whereas Harris can never have had an idea in his head, and Smythe has none but our ideas.

But it was not because of his stage-management that the British public stood by Irving — it was not because he was made out to be a white-winged angel that he was knighted — the first actor to receive knighthood (and "they'll knight no other actor after me," I heard him say) — it was not for these, and because "so gentlemanly," that he was finally laid to rest in Westminster Abbey.

He endured all these things, much in the same spirit in which he endured the applause of the public. It is well to be clear about this.

Those who would teach future generations to slight his memory — a thing they must assuredly fail to do — would do it by teaching these future generations to look upon him as a poor actor, deficient in knowledge, without intuition; one who, by surrounding himself with every kind of fortuitous aid, propped up a something-nothing without which he would have come tardy off indeed. A farcical picture, unavoidably so, because invented by a *farceur*.

I have, therefore, thought it as well to insist on the fact that Irving thought *only* as an actor, never, as we say, "as an artist," "as a producer," "as a dramatist," or as anything else whatever. Even off the stage he thought as an actor.

Which would you have the supreme actor do — think and feel like Molière or like Comrade Bernard Shaw? Molière was an actor; Mr. Shaw maybe can act a little, for all I know, but doesn't and hasn't. Molière did. "Oh," you say, "but Molière was a bad actor." (I have heard a French actress say so.) Now, how do you know that? What is it to be a good actor, if it isn't to go onto the stage — work there for ten years and there write plays for himself and company, and such attractive plays that they please the critical and the general public, such great plays that they live on into our time, and testify how brilliant they are, and how theatrical. What actor is better known than Molière — is Shakespeare? Anyhow for my part I think that close after these names comes Irving's.

To resume. Irving was not primarily a producer or a stage-manager. He was neither a writer, a designer nor a musician, nor did he ever claim to be a singer or a showman. There is a heap that he was not, and yet if called on to do anything the Theatre demands, he could, as a rule, do it and do it perfectly: but he did it as an actor, and once more let us rehearse it, for one actor — himself.

This would be an inexcusable thing in any Billy Browne or Sam Smythe, for the Brownes and Smythes are at most but little nobodies, and their egotism is objectionable — but the more egoistical a great artist is, the better for everyone else. Everyone else is the excuse: it's not better for him — but it is blessed indeed for the others.

Thus much said, let us see when it was that Irving first began to stage-manage plays. This will prove a very difficult question for the historian to answer, if he forgets for a moment that Irving was actor and only actor. That well remembered, he will then note with a gleam of joy that Irving began to stage-manage or produce as early as 1864, when he was playing the leading rôles.

Irving was not a producer in the sense that Reinhardt and I are producers. We can less easily explain to you the slow evolution of the actor-stage-manager than could Gillette, Sothern, Arliss or Barrymore. Whether they will ever do so is quite another matter — but they could do it if they would. Their difficulty is that it's all too simple to explain. The job grows, with an actor manager whose main thought is himself; and to describe any such simple process would be very difficult. To do so properly, he would have to confess all his own weaknesses, in order to show why it is he is obliged to prop up one weakness here and another there, and how he does it — so it is unlikely that any successful actor will ever bother to do this. It is a book we stand in need of — but it had best be an absolutely honest confession: no more bunkum do we want added to the history of the humbug of the stage.

II

IT WAS the custom in and before Irving's day for the actor of the chief rôle, whoever he might be, when rehearsing a new play, to call the tune and set the pace. So that Irving, who since 1864 had been playing the chief rôles, had also slowly developed the craft of producing a play, side by side with the craft of acting it. By the time he came to produce *The Bells,* he had been some eight years an actor producer, and as a production *The Bells* was a masterpiece, as well as a masterly performance.

The craft of the actor producer is this. He reads a play: he comes to know the play well; and then the idea of the play as a theatre-piece strikes him, with himself and his limitations and powers well in his mind's eye — well centred. This *idea* which strikes him may be a right or a wrong one from the dramatist's point of view (recall the great Frédéric in *Robert Macaire,* and Sothern in *Our American Cousin*), but, right or wrong, this is how it strikes him, and it is this impression that he decides to

put over the footlights, so that it shall strike the spectators in the same way and amaze their very faculties of
eyes and ears. Especially of melodrama is this true, and
melodrama is one of the best kinds of modern drama.

Having decided on his line of action, he brings up half
his forces — the other half he keeps in reserve — and,
strengthening the weak spots in the play and in his own
personality by expressive happenings in the crowd (which
is also acting), and still other bare spots by expressive
scene and lighting (which is also acting), he gradually
makes invulnerable and fool-proof all that before was
rather weak and impossible.

Then he brings all this into action, advances on the
audience, and captures the town.

That's about all it is.

As You Like It or *The Bells* can be produced not one
way only, but many — the process is generally identical.
Which interpretation is the best one, depends upon the
actor producer and on the spectators. (There are yet
other ways — for example, the way of the producer who
is *not* an actor in the piece; the Duke of Meiningen's
way.) Yes, much depends upon who are the spectators:
for a cultured Southern Chinese might witness a good
London performance of a drama without being in any
way moved or interested — he might, in fact, be puzzled
and rather shocked: a cultured Englishman might leave
at the end of the first act during a performance of Seami's
Robe of Feathers, in Tokio, bored to death. So we have
to be well aware of our spectators and who those spectators are, and even though we may learn to carry them

away, we have first to know them and *get* them. In Japan a producer may get them in a way no producer would dream of attempting in our land, and *vice versa*. All things are presumably fair in love and producing.

As A producer of Shakespeare and Tennyson plays, Henry Irving was indebted to E. W. Godwin, of whom Sir H. Beerbohm Tree wrote, in 1900, that his production of *The Merchant of Venice,* at the Prince of Wales Theatre, London, in 1875, *" was the first production in which the modern spirit of stage-management asserted itself."* But then we must not forget that Irving was already a great stage-manager, since in 1871 he had produced *The Bells,* in which " the modern spirit of stage-management " perhaps asserted itself less than did the ancient and modern genius of the actor, but which, for all this, was a perfect piece of stage-management.

I have also seen it implied, if not stated, that without Ellen Terry to help him in the production of a play, his productions would not have been so beautiful — I am sure this is incorrect. Ellen Terry was, like Irving, all actress: with a woman's taste for lovely things, responding to music, to painting, to sculpture and architecture as a highly-gifted woman of temperament ever responds to these things — but creative as a stage-producer, no. Irving was very creative as a producer. But Irving thought less in terms of scene and costume, period, atmosphere, manners, and customs, than in terms of melodramatic effect. His productions of *The Bells, The Lyons Mail, Louis XI, Olivia,* and much of *Faust,* were essentially Irvingesque, and indebted to no one.   To me, these were the productions which revealed the highest point of his genius as a stage-manager.

I, too, have produced some plays and operas, and without question, I feel that it is due to his curious example that today I am held abroad to be — may I say — rather a good producer.

I think that this is perhaps worth explaining rather more in detail.

I find that it is only the more melodramatic plays and operas which appeal to me as a producer. I will turn a hundred times to the consideration of *Macbeth* [1] as a production, rather than once to the *Midsummer Night's Dream,* which is supposed to offer such unlimited opportunities for scenical effect. I really do not warm to scenical effect — scenery bores me — the pictorial leaves me unmoved — dramatic effect is the only thing which moves me. Because *St. Joan* or *Henry V* are to be set in a gorgeous period where the banners and the coats of arms and silks and fine array of the times enchant every " decorator," is, alas! no cause for enchantment in me. I am, therefore, no decorator — I am a stage-manager, for all the fairies' dresses of all the Midsummer Dreams in the world cannot give me one thrill equal to that which I receive when I think of the figure of Banquo as he passes to his room, the moon gone down, and asks what time it is; or when Hamlet, pointing into space, whispers:

---

[1] Maybe it seems strange to one or two of my readers that I speak of *Macbeth* as melodramatic — but then I rate melodrama at its best very highly — *Othello, Richard III, Hamlet,* all seem to me to be big and noble melodramas. There is much melodrama in Dante's *Divina Commedia.*

"Do you see nothing there?" To handle a good spectacle is, of course, a good bit of fun, but drama in action is the only thrill.

And it is only drama or opera in action that I care to work at on the stage of a modern theatre — and when I do so, I go at it as seriously as a judge . . . not in the playful way. The playful producer has made a little name for himself, which I hope will never grow less, but I can never be sympathetic to that manner of producing which makes a jest of the stage. It is derived from Oscar Wilde and Beerbohm Tree, two men of genius and wit who were both sufficiently remarkable to be allowed their occasional bit of fun. This "bit of fun" was a huge joke to Tree, whose productions were weighty and astonishing efforts in glorious spectacular pageant. But if that *bit* of fun of a man with a real touch of genius like Tree, lends some sparkle to a piece, not so a whole evening of it, in which the stage is turned into a butt for superficial cleverness to aim at — and that cleverness the funny ideas of the little director of the theatre.

A Pantomime Rehearsal, done so well in 1891, was an amusing little skit in which we were supposed to witness the excruciating difficulties amateurs get into when preparing a Christmas show. It was this piece which gave our modern jokers their cue.

The playful producer enjoys nothing so much as raising a laugh from his public at the expense of the stage. This belongs to the province of the circus, and when a clown of position and weight, like Frattelini or Grock, taps the scenery to show that it is only canvas or three-ply boards, well and good — but when the kind of thing is joked about all through a series of productions running for five or six years, one is not only apt to be bored, but to feel that it reveals a pitiful ambition in the producer who uses it.

I have touched on this jesting with theatre things by one or two theatre men of the day, because there was nothing Irving could tolerate less than that.

To him, as a producer, and as one of the craft, whatever belonged to the stage was to be held in reverence by those who used it. No stage king was to take off his crown of pasteboard, turn down one of the spikes, and look a mirthless witticism such as: " Crikey! it's only cardboard! " Irving cared passionately for our calling — these jokers only care to flirt with it. Some of us, who derive from his school, follow him anyhow in this, and I have felt it right of us to follow Irving's lead still, and that we do better to err on the side of being even a trifle too serious about it all, rather than not serious enough.

III

So THEN Irving, who was a great actor, was also a great stage-manager, a good producer, a good director of a theatre.

He was a selfish man,[2] and it is ridiculous to try to pic-

---

[2] " *He was a selfish man.*" An old friend of mine, whose opinion I value, on reading this in *The Times,* where some pages of this book first appeared, wrote me that the use of the word " selfish " was more than likely to create a wrong impression. He pointed out to me that, while later on I state that *" Irving was a selfish man without a jot of self-interest,"* I seem to forget that a selfish man, as generally understood, is a man who is only self-interested, and that most people use the word as the worst term of reproach.

ture him as thinking over-considerately of others, or of the
other arts — of theories, and of the blessedness of a perfect stage — for he had no illusions about these things
after he had become Irving, in that memorable and shining year of grace, 1871, when he created the rôle of
Mathias in *The Bells*.

Irving was a selfish man without a jot of self-interest.
He was without consideration for anyone else, never
spared himself, and would never unprovoked hurt anyone.
He had a failing (I suppose it must be called a weakness),
and that was that he too often credited others with his own

I wish no one to suppose I should use it in that sense here — yet I must
use the word. For I mean this — that Irving in his theatre was what
Napoleon was in the midst of his army. Irving was sole ruler of the Theatre
of England, from 1871 till his death. No ruler is either fool enough or
cruel enough to be an altruist. What he cares most for — cares solely for —
is the thing over which he has come to rule. Irving's kindness was well
known, his patience was astounding; but patient and kind as he was to us all,
he thought for himself and of himself: never spared himself — spared us very
often — and yet more often spared no one.

His will was all that mattered at the Lyceum Theatre. The man who
wills the rest of mankind to do as he wishes, is a selfish man — with or
without personal interest, benefiting much or not at all. I object to calling
a spade anything but a spade — but I object more to finding a spade something to apologize for. So the word "selfish" must stand. But let no
farceur who hides a far greater and a far meaner selfishness under a breezy
manner, attempt to make out that Irving was meanly selfish or arrogantly
selfish.

So devoted was Irving to our stage, that he really was innocently selfish.
My mother often used to say, with a lovely twinkle in her eyes, "Yes, yes —
were I to be run over by a steam-roller tomorrow, Henry would be deeply
grieved; would say quietly, 'What a pity.' — and would add, after two
moments' reflection, 'Who is there — er — to go on for her tonight?'"
She knew he was selfish for our British Theatre's sake — that he placed the
stage above the ground, as a priest does his church, and that whether he
dropped dead or she, or "poor old Daddy Howe" or "young Ted," the play
must go on.

That's selfish — that's a wise selfishness: but the man who thinks and
acts ruthlessly like that, is just the man the *farceur* will be down on and
misrepresent, bearing false witness against him which will be believed — so
mind *you* don't believe that testimony — it's false.

The Lyceum Theatre in 1817. *Drawn by E. Burney. Engraved by J. Stow.*

powers of endurance and self-criticism. He had no tol-
eration for any signs of feebleness in himself, and he
credited us all with a like capacity for self-discipline.

He did not always see that most of us contained too
little of that demon which requires so much effort to subdue. I think that to the end he liked to credit us all
with the possession of a demon or two. Anyway, he was
always hopeful.

For the actors of his troupe he had a respect, provided they could come on precisely at the third beat of the
line or go off at the tenth — but if they could not do that,
he was apt to wonder what the devil it was they could do.
Then would his good mind commune for an instant
with his good heart, and he would mutter to himself: " I
suppose I pay him in-ad-e-quate-ly? " He must have
forgotten that, only too often, he paid everyone more
than they asked; but for all this, when puzzled at
the lack of quick wits, his first thought would be
£.s.d., and: " Yes — give him another five pounds a
week — fat cats hunt better than lean. I was a lean cat
once."

Those lean days of his had been terrible enough to him,
and he supposed that to anyone with a scrap of the soul
of God Almighty in him, the lean days would be equally
terrible. Alas, this was but an innocent way of looking
at it — it was seeing through a very good heart to see
things that way. For the good old actor, the tough old
boot of an actor, the fat old matter-of-fact buffer of those
days, was little troubled by any over-weight of God
Almighty; what he troubled about was to do just as little

as he possibly could manage, and get a rise of salary for doing it.

In the Lyceum Theatre I recall certain actors, those who were always with him (many of whom have now passed away), who worked exceedingly well — very hard — and all for Hecuba and Henry. The one I shall ever remember best is Mr. John Archer; and yet how many are there who have heard of the actor Mr. John Archer?

Mr. John Archer played the important parts in the more important productions. An important part is like the leg of a table — not much to look at. Irving, when casting around in his mind for someone to fill one of these important three or four rôles — someone to rely on — thought quite often of Archer. An important rôle, to a serious actor manager, is that character which comes into the play at a dangerous moment — at the moment when he (the actor manager) is on the stage and about to do some very difficult trick. I use the word "trick" because it is well known that the assistant of a skilled conjurer must be no fool — must be able to keep his head — must remember the almost trifling things he is told to do, and must never bungle these. So it was with the conjurer Irving. A good actor was one who could do the bit he was given to do, and do it as he was told to do it. Let all the critics who failed to understand Irving, fail not to remember that this is one of the most ancient traditions known to masters and apprentices. We apprentices in Irving's time were at our best when, like this faithful old John Archer, we did our bit on the night as we were told to do it by the Chief. Archer was all right on the night — and Archer went down to the grave practically unknown. That's a good soldier, isn't it? And no record of Henry Irving is complete which withholds a tribute to this little old man. Yet every record that I have seen is silent about him.

Among the important parts which Archer played were these:

In *The Bells*	*Mesmerist.*
In *The Merchant of Venice*	*Tubal.*
In *The Lyons Mail*	*Fouinard.*
In *Louis XI*	*Oliver le Dain.*
In *Richard III*	*Sir William Catesby.*
In *Macbeth*	*Second Witch.*
In *Othello*	*Lodovico.*

In 1892, Mr. John Archer would have been chosen to play the small part of *Cromwell* in *Henry VIII* — but I was younger, and it needed a younger man for the part. Besides, I was fast becoming, by that time, one of the reliables — beginning to stand still — " Keeps out of the way — useful in . . . er . . . a sense." So I was chosen, and Irving once wrote, in a rash but kindly moment, that he even missed me when another took my place. Conceive the delirium of my joy — I, at last, a table-leg! that was indeed happiness.

Let no one suppose that he meant more than does a good mechanic, who discovers one day a new brass handle on one of his taps. He notes the loss — he muses on the old tap — no more, no less — turns to the new one — tries it — " All right."

When Martin Harvey was no longer there, after 1899,

to play *Joliquet* in *The Lyons Mail,* I do not doubt that Irving was more deeply grieved than if he had lost a couple of thousand pounds; but the most that he said probably resolved itself into: " Pity the young man wasn't there tonight."

Martin Harvey was one of that small group of devoted actors who had been with him since 1885; Harvey only left him in 1899, six years before Irving's death.

Next to Archer in value, I would place Miss Pauncefort, who until her death in 1895, was always Irving's *Catherine* in *The Bells,* his *Gertrude* in *Hamlet,* from 1874, and his *Emilia* in *Othello,* from 1881.

Another trusty and trusted actor was Frank Tyars, who acted under Irving from 1877 till his death in 1905. Another was Sam Johnson, who had played with him in 1856, when he first went on the stage — an able actor, but of course not inspired . . . it was not inspiration Irving looked for . . . for the reason I am now coming to.

If anyone had shown inspiration in Irving's company (and I believe the whole company will agree with me when I say that no one did this but Ellen Terry — her sole apology being that she couldn't help it), he would promptly have been sacked.

Ellen Terry only retained her place in Irving's company because it was plain to see what efforts she was making to suppress herself — and having that tact of the clever woman, she did really keep her place.

To Irving, inspiration had so often proved itself to be merely a way of spoiling something. He preferred a little calculation in us, for he it was who would inspire things

— " get on — get on." This perhaps sounds strange to
you — especially to you who may be reading this in 1979,
when surely all of us who saw Irving will be dead and
gone. But it is the truth — Irving's immense success for
thirty years was designed on a very small piece of paper
— with space to hold just two words — " Henry Irving "
. . . that stood for concentrated inspiration — and the
only thing that stands in need of is solid, matter-of-fact
support — we tried to support him, we table-legs.

But I do not wish to give a wrong impression — to picture the entire Lyceum company, from 1871 to 1902, as
a crowd of dummies.

There were celebrities among us. For one season, Sir
Squire Bancroft performed with us: for two seasons, Mr.
Fred Terry. Sir Johnstone Forbes-Robertson seems to
have been engaged three times by Irving. Sir George
Alexander seems to have been at the Lyceum, playing important parts, from 1881 to 1882, and then again from
1885 to 1887.

Other actors, less celebrated, but never to be looked
upon as dummies, were Mr. William Mackintosh, Mr.
Wenman, Mr. Fernandez, Mr. Frank Cooper, Mr. Gerald
Laurence, Mr. Macklin, Mr. Alfred Bishop, and Mr.
Arthur Stirling . . . the list of important actors can be
drawn up any day by reference to the list at the end of a
delightful book by Austin Brereton, called The Lyceum
and Henry Irving, published in 1903, by Lawrence and
Bullen.

But besides the celebrated and the important, there was
the Irving body-guard — the table-legs — call them what

you will; and though Ellen Terry was celebrated and a genius, I know that she prefers to be in this group — so I place her there. With her is Sir Arthur Wing Pinero — as loyal to Irving as to the group, and unique, since on leaving his training-ground, the Lyceum (1877 to 1881), he before long became the foremost dramatist of Great Britain.

Around these two great names, E. T.'s and A. W. P.'s, are a number of wonderful fellows and excellent ladies — old Mr. Henry Howe and young Norman Forbes — Howe, well known even in Macready's time, was intelligent and delightful. My dear old John Archer or Mr. Tapping, besides being intelligent and delightful, were *essential:* what that signifies God only knows, today or at any time. The essential men, great or small, are paid least, do most, and are known not at all — are often in their wrong place, but always on the spot — want little, grumble a good deal, give much, since they give all they have.

"That's all very well," someone may say to you tomorrow, "but it's not exact." The passion the prejudiced have for being exact is commendable. You will hear more from such an one. He will say, "Irving *had* to take these people, the Archers and Tappings, because he couldn't get anyone better" — which, it seems to me, will do quite well for a reason.

For it is quite true . . . Irving could not get anyone *better*. Had he engaged Mackintosh (who was a remarkable actor) to perform the part of the *Mesmerist* in 1871 and 1880, instead of Tapping and Archer, Mackintosh would not have been better, he would have been worse. Again—no one could have been better than Frank Tyars in *The Lyons Mail*—than Tom Reynolds in *The Merchant of Venice,* than A. W. Pinero as *Maynard* in *The Corsican Brothers,* than Mr. Tabb as a *Clerk* in *The Merchant of Venice,* or than Mr. Norman Forbes as the *Student* in *Faust.* Difficult work they had to do, and it was done thoroughly.

All these were small parts, and all had to be as well done as the setting up of this page has been done by Longmans' type-setter—orderly, professional enough, not too much of the craft *displayed*. The type-setter, who doubtless admires some of the work of William Morris, were he to begin Morris-ing here, would successfully queer my pitch. It was our attempt not to spoil the Guvnor's pitch that gives us today the right to be held as a damn good company of actors—spite of anything Mr. Bernard Shaw may have written.

Other names occur to me, amongst H. I.'s *âmes damnées:* Tom Mead, Mr. and Mrs. Lacy, Nellie de Silva, Fuller Mellish, W. Marion, Willa Brown, Belmore, Geoffrey Taylor, Henry Kemble Barnett, Lizzie Archer, Mrs. Tyars, William Farren, Haviland, Yeldham, Black, Edith Craig, and old Allen; I can only think of him as " old Allen "; you see a portrait of him in the painting of Irving as *Dubosc,* by Pryde.

Besides all these, no one is likely to forget the name of William Terriss. William Terriss was the hero of all heroes, the handsomest hero ever seen on a stage, the most manly figure of that time. Very valuable to

Irving. When I was a boy he was a great favourite of mine — he never was too celebrated or too old to stop and talk to young people. I had one or two letters from him, either wishing me a merry Christmas or sending a birthday gift, and all were much like his talk — pessimistic, florid, but delightful: because once one had seen Terriss walking along — erect — head splendidly carried, with brows rather like Buonaparte's, and turning sharply to the right and to the left to face whatever caught his eye; and when one had seen him chatting with others, ever erect, proud, merry, but for all that grave as a guardsman on duty — once one had seen this and experienced the many kind acts he could not help committing, one came to realize that, pen in hand, he felt he had to give you a bit of sound philosophy: and the following extract from one of his letters is typical of all of them. They called him " Breezy Bill," but he was a much deeper, nobler character than that sort of nickname conveys.

. . . hundreds of shirts and one is not content without a score or two more though you can never wear them — no, what we give we enjoy — what we spend we enjoy, but every bob we save we lose. Give me please God a quiet little home unobserved — quiet and alone to pass along this weary road of life which when you get my age you will recognise as a hollow shallow mockery. Taking off your trousers at night and in the morning putting them on again — that's all. All applause is mockery and the noise has scarce died away when those who make it and those for whom it is given are forgotten — Carpe Diem — Enjoy the present. Lay not riches up to yourself in life. A pipe — a rod and line — a good appetite and one friend and you are . . .

The next page I have lost, so I cannot remember what one is when one has these blessings, but I take it, a lucky man. Terriss was very fond of that motto, "*Carpe Diem,*" and ended one of his letters to me: "*and in the dim future give a few thoughts to old Carpe Diem.*" I have given many a thought to him since he died in 1897, but always the thoughts resolved themselves into remembrances of a *young* "Carpe Diem."

IV

IN THE old days, old even to Irving, there was very little ducking to the English public, to the man in the street. Indeed, there was little need to kowtow to him, for in those days he didn't like it. That happy man in the street was privileged to enjoy what he was able to appreciate, provided he was willing to put up with all the discomfort of a more or less ramshackle pit and gallery — he was not any softer than were the benches he sat on — yet he did not grumble.

Nowadays all this is changed, and Irving, at the end of his career, was among those who were obliged to adapt themselves to the change.

The man in the street today has no longer a claim to the street — he is a superior person — so his honourable title has gone; he is now ushered into boxes, stalls, or circle. He dresses up to the new rôle. As we know, he is rapidly becoming all-important.

Outside and inside, he has been tidied up and softened down: he cannot abide a bench, and vastly prefers to sit in comfort. Plays are not less to his liking than Revues

or Variety shows, provided the house be well appointed.
If his wife enjoys other kinds of entertainment, she anyhow thoroughly detests Shakespeare, or anything serious.
He and his wife pay the piper — call the tune — insist on
the ventilation being perfect — the cloak-room superb
— the entrance-hall regal — the passages well furnished
— the carpets thick and soft — the seats downy — the programmes elegantly printed. And the management " *has
pleasure in announcing* " the trash it offers them.

Irving to some extent helped to make this trash popular,
for he could not prevent it. He could not make the laws
— and the laws have allowed both journalism and the
cinema to *cheapen* the mind of the public. Had Irving
gone against the public he might have had to starve.

What can a single man do against millions of his coun-
trymen, bent on levelling things down to the main idea
— material comfort?

" *The Lyceum,*" wrote Mr. William Archer, in 1883, " *is
more than fashionable, it is popular.*" He does not explain why — he seems puzzled. Mr. Irving's " *electricity,*"
i.e. his advertising, is, he thinks, at the bottom of the
business.

But the secret is simple. Irving was one of the first
actors to thoroughly understand the public . . . but thoroughly. A thrill, to be taken in comfort, was what they
asked for, was it — then they should have it. Irving, being
fond of the mysterious, had not watched the Davenport
brothers mystifying England for nothing; and when, in a
moment of youthful fun, he had appeared on the Man-
chester stage and announced that he would unmask these

Davenport brothers, he was within an ace of ruining his career. Having shown how the Davenport brothers did their little trick, he went home to his lodgings, and slowly there dawned an expression on his face . . . a very strange expression. This expression dawned slowly, as he recalled the gaping faces of the sturdy spectators he had that day seen watching him unveil a mystery.

He had not a very great opinion of the public. The booing and the hissing it had subjected him to, had taught him that it was an unreasonable animal — a nervous animal, given to kicking if you showed it a good serious play with very fine playing and without any barn-storming. After all, it was Barry Sullivan at his worst that the unreasoning, unreasonable public loved most.

"But I cannot barn-storm," said Henry Irving to himself. "Besides, I will not. Suppose . . . suppose I mesmerise 'em. That's an idea. Kemble? . . . Kemble was too noble with 'em. Edmund Kean? . . . a ruthless assault! I am not Kean — more like Kemble, perhaps, but er-r — , Kemble — too noble — too noble. Garrick? too long ago — silks and satins — and a damn small city — coffee houses — powder and patches — another age. But Mesmer . . . Mesmer never went on the stage. Joseph Balsamo . . . Cagliostro. Suppose we put *him* on now?" Saying which, Henry Irving with decision went off to bed.

The next morning — the next week — the next years — allowing his mind to rehearse once more the tricks of the Davenport brothers, he saw clearly how gullible was a public which had been allowed to fall in love with itself — and coming by easy stages to the far more profound thoughts of Mesmer, and to the most surprising powers of Cagliostro, and perceiving that he possessed something of these powers too — he made up his mind, and the Rubicon was passed.

These powers of mesmerism he developed in himself to an astonishing degree, and if only a few actors of today would develop a modicum of the dangerous faculty, I think it would greatly increase the enjoyment of those evenings which at present we are forced to pass without too much happiness, in the theatre. We should then perhaps feel something . . . be attracted.

V

" I MADE *them out of a mouthful of air,"* writes the poet of his songs. It is not yet from the four winds which blow round that poet's eyrie that any actor can create beautiful things.

But descending to the actor's lair, we find that he too can make something, if not out of nothing, out of very little — a hat — a box — a pocket handkerchief. He is a great conjurer.

With what an air of mystery and mastery this prestidigitator, Henry Irving, advanced to the persuasive, waltz-like music of the violins, and slowing down as it ceased, inclined his head to us ever so little, and in his first three words, riveted our attention and aroused all the life in us.

"Ladies and gentlemen " — the music steals in again as the baton moves, as we hear the conjurer's voice with an extraordinary precision, telling us that he will produce

Sketch of Henry Irving by Paul Renouard (about 1885).

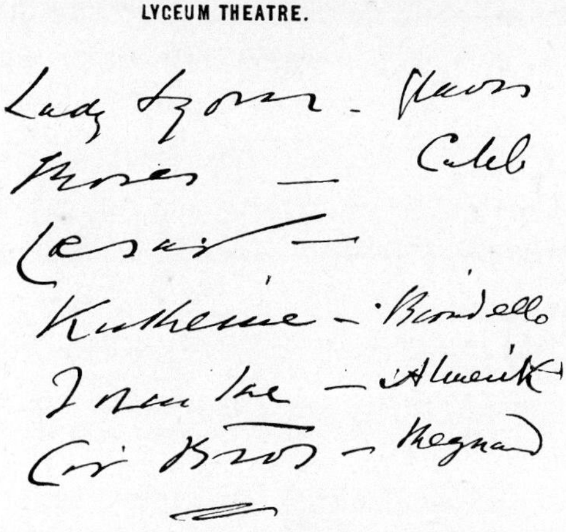
LYCEUM THEATRE.

Note in Irving's handwriting — 1891.

a garden of flowers from a hat. With what a terrible
courtesy he robs us of our ease — how his smiling solem-
nity becomes the few first passes which he makes with his
delicate hand — how the mystery thickens around this
child's play — how sure he seems of winning the trick . . .
his handkerchief suddenly flashes out — it waves faintly,
as though dying; and there is a garden of flowers — and
all out of a hat.

A great believer in puppets, Irving's regret was that in
his theatre they had to be made of flesh and blood: he
never expressed this, but he never failed to feel it.

He engaged actors at from £5 a week to £50, or more.
Seldom gave them less than £5 a week, and that in 1890
— forty years ago.

He rehearsed these actors unceasingly, and tried to make
good marionettes of them: yes, for he enjoyed rehearsing
and attempting this. To work for hours upon his stage
with his actors, scene-painters, carpenters, musicians and
lime-light men, was a joy to him . . . how he ever found
time to study his own rôles was our wonder, for he never
seemed to stop rehearsing the others. But if we had
guessed that the rôles came to him while he was rehearsing
us all, I think we should not have been far wrong —
though of course I do not know about this.

At rehearsals he would waste no time — but we often
wasted it for him. I remember that an actor who was to
play *Kent* in *King Lear*,[3] wasted about an hour at one of
the rehearsals in the vain attempt to make the gesture of
tripping someone up with his foot — to make this at the

---

[3] I think he did not play the part at performance.

right moment, on the right syllable of the right word. The line was: "*Nor tripped neither you base football player*," and the actor made sundry jabs with first one foot and then the other, always on the wrong word. Irving held that there was a right word on which to do it, while this actor, unconscious that such a thing as the right word existed, would try it first on the word "*nor*," then on the word "*tripped*," or after the word "*neither*," or on the word "*base*" — and finally on the first syllable of the word "*player*." On these words he would make a rough jab with his foot. What Irving was telling him to do, was to make a very slight motion, brushing the ground with his right foot (chiefly the toe part of the said foot) on the first syllable of the word "*neither*," and on no other syllable — no other word. Over and over we went — "Nor tripped *nei*ther" etc., and not once did he get it right. (He was not, I may add, one of the "table-legs" — a "table-leg" would have caught the notion.)

I happened to be playing the part of *Oswald,* the one to be tripped, and so I was there all the time — luckily doing my bit rather well — and helping to the best of my ability.

"Try it again, my boy," says the voice of the Chief to the player of *Kent;* and he tried it, and down I went, rather neatly for me (for I had done it by then some thirty times within forty-five minutes). We had to pretend to trip and pretend to be tripped — to act it — and the actor of *Kent* simply couldn't see why he should come swish with his foot on the word "*neither*"— on its first syllable. He got it at last — rather roughly put a kind of swing to his foot, somewhere near the right moment. What this illustrates I'm not quite sure. It could serve to show how patient Irving was — how concerned about a trifle — how passionately fond of rhythm — how dull the actor — or how obstinate — or how paralysed. But what it may stand for here is the intense joy I experienced at the time, and still experience to-day, to think, to feel certain, great Heavens! to know that I was actually doing *my* bit just as he wanted it.

In this same play, *King Lear,* I had received from stage-manager Irving, the key to the character of *Oswald,* as I was to play it. But how he told me . . . with what a way! When I received my script, I read the lines I had to speak, and I wondered what the devil it was all about. "Oswald — a Steward — hmm" — my mind went at once towards thoughts of Atlantic liners — and that made me feel no better. "Oswald" — the name began to hypnotize me. All I could do was to go around puzzling and murmuring: "Oswald . . . Oswald" — and I had one rather shrewd idea, which was, that before very long Irving would tell me exactly who Oswald was. He told us all who we were, why, and what we had to do.

It was the first rehearsal. "Well, my boy," he said — only he said, "Welllll, me buy," which was a hundred times better, of course, being proper old English — but I will translate as I go along. "Well, my boy," said Irving to me, as he passed me and stopped — " err — m — er — this — er — part (pat, he said) this pat — err — m, what do you — er — make of it?" All I could do was to murmur and suggest that the part seemed to me to be "barbaric " — at which he gave an almost imperceptible leap in the air, and quietly went on, " Yes — barbaric — barbaric — yes — err," and by this time he was warming up — pinched his nose very slightly at the nostril — stopped dead — was about to move off — riveted me with the kindest of stern glances, and said simply " Malvolio " — and on he passed.

With *that* in my pocket I knew what to do, and didn't hesitate. He helped me just as he would help himself — to escape from the terrible uncertainty that Shakespeare gets us into about so many of his minor characters, and to raise a small unimportant part to a rôle of the first magnitude — by simplifying.

When Irving gave me permission to join the Harvey-Haviland company, of which you may have heard, he took the trouble to write down on a scrap of paper which parts he wished me to play. I reproduce it here.

And when, a while later, I went on another tour, and wanted to borrow some dresses from the Lyceum, Irving, always ready to help anyone about the work, asked me what kind of costume I thought of wearing as *Claude Melnotte* in the last scene of *The Lady of Lyons*. As usual, I made a mistake — Irving's questions were generally intended to help by drawing out the wrong reply, so that he might plant the right one in. In this instance, I remember I suggested wearing the proper uniform of the regiment to which *Claude Melnotte* belonged — but to my astonishment, Irving wouldn't say yes to this, and suggested something so meaningless to me, that even till now I do not know what it was he was getting at; not joking, that I know — for practical jokes about the work were unknown to Irving — a bit of fun about the work was not possible to him — it would have been " damn silly." But this, I recall it, was altogether *incorrect,* this costume he suggested — just as when it came to *Cymbe-line,* the leopard-skin he gave me to wear (in spite of Alma Tadema's presence, and Tadema was a stickler for correct costume) was utterly incorrect: the old black velvet suit I wore in *Henry VIII,* when playing *Cromwell* to his *Wolsey,* was equally incorrect. What seemed fitting, that was best, with him. All the correctness in the world was not worth a fig to Irving, unless it *seemed* all right: one supposes that everyone who thinks at all about stage work will come to think in this way, but it is not so very often that this point of development is reached.

The stories we tell in our books about Irving's capacity as a stage-director, hardly do him justice; for the kind of thing we tell about is, how he listened to six different kinds of bells being rehearsed, and actually hit on those he wanted; how he had some lights turned up and others turned down, and a wonderful effect was the result.

All such trifles he certainly attended to, and it brought about a perfection he desired, but these matters were all in the day's work.

While preparing for the production of *Henry VIII,* in June 1891, Irving wrote to my mother:

. . . I have come across some wonderful books today at Quaritch's, and I have been buried in 'em. NM——— (a scene-painter working for Henry VIII), in a week — with 2 boys to assist him — had stuck together two bits of cardboard

and called it a scene. He has no more invention than a rabbit
— and I'd given him a picture too. But I was so disgusted
. . . etc., etc. . .

One is apt to hear just a little too often the old-fashioned
scene-painters' version of how much Irving admired their
work, so this is not a little refreshing.

There was one scene-painter, Mr. Harker, who in 1924
issued a book called *Studio and Stage,* telling us of many
an interesting fact — but he allowed his fancy to run away
with him, and he grew excessively cross with a certain
Exhibition of Theatrical Art held in 1922 at the Victoria
and Albert Museum. It was a very serious exhibition of
the best work — the best work — of all the nations, yet at
which even the late Mr. W. B. Walkeley thought it wise
to sneer.

Mr. Harker enlisted Sir Johnstone Forbes-Robertson,
Mr. Fred Terry, and others, twenty-five in all, to agree
how clever and inventive he was — which is quite proper
and true — but to add that the new men were "im-
posters," which is not the truth. He even persuaded Sir
Arthur Wing Pinero to write against us all. I could not
quarrel with Pinero — he is an old Lyceum man, one of
the very loyalest.

But it was an ill-advised book, for Harker was always
well paid by Irving, Tree, Alexander, and others. He had
made a pretty penny out of painting scenes to order, and
deserved every penny — whereas the majority of the artists
exhibiting at the Victoria and Albert Museum, men of the
very first rank, had another motive for working. They
had practically done as Irving wanted: were not in busi-

ness nor out for business, but in revolt against the stupidity of the stage. No one had paid them to revolt — and they had shown invention in their work, and had done it in the interests of the Theatre, not from self-interest.

I SUPPOSE few actors have acted in darker scenes than Irving. At the Lyceum the lights were often turned very low. It was from Irving that I learnt to plunge my scenes in a good deal too much gloom — but the fault must not be laid at his door. Irving could not really be expected to establish, out of his own purse, a school for Theatrical Art, with picked masters for acting, speaking, singing, dancing, scenography and all the minor crafts; but I will come to this matter of Schools, awhile later.

It took me a long time to realize that I should not copy the faults of a man of genius — and when I did realize this, I began to do some better work. It took me long to break free from the glorious influence, but I always have loved to be Irving's pupil, and I count on his help to this day.

SCHOOLS AND MASTERS

SCHOOLS

In Irving's time no school for the Theatre existed but the rough and ready one of hard experience; and though Irving at one time (in 1894), held that "for actors, the advantage of a permanent school would be invaluable," he meant only such a school as the Comédie Française once offered, with its Conservatoire as annex — nothing meaner.

Those who have done me the courtesy to read my books, may recall that I have touched on this question of a school: but of a thorough school for the study of the Theatre and all its crafts — not acting alone — and having seen some of these preparatory places in Europe (not the Paris Conservatoire), I am struck with one thing common to most of them. They push ahead; they are not afraid of advancing towards a new Theatre — prejudice does not stifle them — they are not antagonistic both to new and old ideas: our one institution in England unfortunately is. I know of this, for this institution is curiously antagonistic to all the traditions I care for, and all that I have striven for.

Irving told me the way I was to go, and I follow strictly along his path. If my innovations are rejected, and rejected with passionate prejudice, as I know they are by some schools in England, such scholars are directly opposed to progress along the lines of the ancient traditions — and such schools, if left as they are, can but continue to do harm, and thus delay the progress we look for.

The permanent school that Irving, in 1894, felt would be invaluable, was to be no little place for beginners. He had no liking for the sort of thing which is too often done to-day. And what is done, you ask? This is what is done. Enthusiasts — beginners — pay fees to study the whole art of the Theatre, and are given lessons by able or by indifferent teachers. At the end of a very brief period, the school finds some of them a job in one of the hundred theatres which are ever on the look-out for "a bit of ability." That's the standard all round — "a bit of ability, a bit of training" — and that standard will not do. On the other hand, I know of a few good schools. "Tell us of these," you ask, and I will with pleasure — but not here, for here we are not concerned with my idea of a good school, but with Irving's.

The school Irving had in mind was a place at least as good as any of the schools of architecture and music: a place where men and women eager to do well should be trained by the best masters until they were sound, reliable executants. Skilled actors and stage-managers — skilled craftsmen of all kinds, skilled scenic men, singers and dancers — maybe even skilled dramatists — would have come from such a school as Irving had in mind; progress and not prejudice would have been its watchword, and had it been established twenty years ago, even ten years ago, the British Theatre would already be feeling the value of such an institution.

No such school exists, and no such school existed when Irving as a young man needed it. He had to learn as he went along, and he devised many a good thing from the good and bad which he picked up in the bitter school of experience. But then he was a man with purpose, application, and genius.

We had no " school " proper at the Lyceum Theatre. One of the most painful moments of cramming that I can remember was when, in 1889, (my first London appearance on the stage), Irving put me into the hands of M. Léon Espinosa, the elder [1] — a little man — a great master of the dance, of about five feet in height, with a marvellous head, and of the quickest intelligence; one who had known Alexandre Dumas *père* — it seemed incredible, but was true — who had, so the great little man told me, been used by Dumas as a walking-stick when he walked out in the Champs Elysées, leaning on little Espinosa's shoulder.

This amazing Dancer of genius took me into the empty Green Room at the Lyceum during a rehearsal of *The Dead Heart,* and there showed me how a young man of the eighteenth century (I was to act one in fourteen days from then) would behave when on the spree. I was to pretend to be a dashing young buck of 1789, by doing such and such and such. He was explicit: he was excellent: he indeed *was* a young man of the eighteenth century — in face, in gesture, in a score of brilliant little ways — he gave me a perfect performance. But whereas he had taken about forty to fifty years to acquire this wonderful tech-

[1] He died in 1903 — his son carries on the great tradition.

nique, I was supposed to acquire the same thing in about three quarters of an hour. Painful, for one should have three years' technical training before being asked to do a hundred bits of by-play as though he were already a highly-skilled performer.

Irving could not stop in his rehearsals to teach us how to act, as a trainer trains pupils. He could and did give us ideas — mostly wasted on us — and he would show us over and over again how to do what he wanted us to do — but after a time his teaching more often than not amounted to, " Hurry up my boy — get along — get along " — and that sometimes during a performance.

Had he stopped to teach us, he would have been forced to give up the Lyceum Theatre and to open a college — to the immense advantage of this generation, and to the bitter disappointment of his own.

I have sometimes wondered whether, if out of the 20,000 hours — about four and a half years — which in the course of twenty years, he had given to playing the host, Irving had devoted, say, half of this time to his Lyceum school — a school which never existed, but which might have existed, had it occurred to him to establish it — I sometimes wonder if the time would have been ill spent.

But it is more than likely that even 10,000 hours robbed from Irving's entertainment of others, would have meant to him an earlier death. I think it would have exhausted him to instruct, whereas it rested him to act the host — and then, at these dinners, banquets, and convivial meetings, he never lost an opportunity of studying a face — a gesture — sometimes a whole person, and thus teaching himself how to act. Bram Stoker tells us in his book that it was at a social function that Irving came across the very man he was looking for as model for his *Digby Grant* in *Two Roses*. This model was the Chevalier Wikoff.

Another reason why Irving would not have had a school is, that he always believed in paying those who worked for him, and paying highly; and to pay people who were still at school would have seemed to him ridiculous — and on the other hand, to have allowed people onto his stage who were not paid, would have been out of the question.

But for all that, I very much regret that later on in his life, say in 1902, the year the Lyceum was taken from him, he did not found the school of which the dramatic art in England still stands in the utmost need.

But while Irving had no schooling, he had masters, and their influence on his work can be traced.

MASTERS

" WHAT was it Garrick did in the Play Scene in *Hamlet* ? " — is what nearly every actor asks himself when preparing to play the part. " And Kean, and Kemble — what did they do — and how did they do it ? " And later in the day he will go to see a fellow-actor, and " What was it Kemble did in this scene ? " he asks.

" Well, Boaden says . . ."

Or if the reply is not what Boaden said, it will be " There is a report handed down by Everard " (or by Smith, or someone), " to the effect that when Garrick cried out ' *the mouse-trap,*' he struck this attitude " — and here the informant strikes said attitude.

Sometimes the information will be a great deal better than that — a very great deal better — but when all is said and done, the passing along of a tradition is a very difficult thing to do successfully. So much drops by the way. For example, the oral tradition about Mrs. Siddons and *Lady Macbeth's* sleep-walking is all contradictory — and the pictures all contradict one another, too. Here she is still, never moves — there she is rushing around. Now which was it? One report tells you, " Always kept moving her hands, as though washing them " : another tells you, " Acted it all with her face." So really an actor can learn little from hearing what was done. And yet no actor in the traditional rôles need bother to do anything other than what was done before; but what he had best be sure of doing is, to do the same thing *differently.* Irving did what Kean and others have done in *Shylock* — *Lear* — *Othello* but did it differently: and now and again he invented, as when he played *Mathias,* in *The Bells,* where he invented the whole thing.

Who helped Irving to become a great actor?

This is not unimportant, though it has not yet been thoroughly gone into, and I shall only be able to touch on it here.

First to his help came the old actors and their tradition. This he learnt well. It had been handed down to him by word of mouth from actor to actor, and some of it had been recorded in books by Lichtenberg, Heine,

Byron, Lamb, Boaden, Hazlitt, Kirkman, and a dozen more.

Secondly there is the help rendered him by Ellen Terry. Here we must go very carefully. The help rendered was incalculable, and to estimate it properly, not at all easy. She helped him with a sympathy born of a great and lasting affection: with an understanding born of appreciation for his immense powers: and with long years of — shall we say — not bad advice. But she no more helped make Irving the actor he became in 1871, than Josephine helped Napoleon to be Buonaparte. Neither did she invent a production for or with him. He did that, and then, showing it to her bit by bit, would ask her opinion. As she says in her memoirs, he was always certain of what he wanted — had no doubts — but liked to take her suggestions wherever possible. " Without Ellen Terry, no Irving possible " is as foolish in implication as to say that without Irving, Ellen Terry would never have been the actress she was. It was a splendid partnership, in the sense that she was herself and he himself, and he without any question the leader.

The worst of it is that some men have a way of going on and on — no stop until they drop — and he was one of these. She could not do that — and she tired a little of the determined advance of a man beaten down by adversity. Never a failure — but growing older he went on slower — and less mindful of obstacles . . . and went through them to his death. She would — who knows — have liked him to change his course — and she, too, felt she was growing no younger — she who was ever young. And so on he

Interior of the New Queen's Theatre, Long Acre, London, in 1867. In this theatre Irving and Ellen Terry acted together for the first time, in December 1867. Irving continued to act here until March 1869.

went, and that took him north — so we can put it — and she was obliged to stay where she was, in the south. Never a quarrel did these two have. Some there were who would say to H. I., " Why Ellen Terry? " Some there were who would scribble to E. T., " Why Henry? " It really made no difference in the long run. We all of us have our path — and on it we must stay — you and I and even the lamp-lighter. How wonderful if for ten years we have one companion on our beat — if for twenty years, what a miracle . . . and for twenty-three years Irving and Ellen Terry went on together.

I have never heard her speak of any man with such admiration, affection, and respect combined, as I heard her, for years, daily saying the loveliest things of Irving. And no one is keener to enjoy such thrilling words than a young man — nor can anyone quicker detect the true from the false. I heard glorious oratorios about him — would that now I could even hum one bar of one of these.

So that was help. But there were deeper influences on his own personal work. Remember that before Irving and my mother were at work together at the Lyceum, he had already created *Mathias* (*The Bells*), *Charles the First*, *Lesurques* and *Dubosc* (*Lyons Mail*), *Philip of Spain* (*Queen Mary*), *Louis XI*, and had produced *Hamlet*, *Macbeth*, *Richard III*, and *Richelieu*, playing the title-rôles. Who then was it from whom he derived: who helped him thus in these productions and in these rôles?

Charles Kean, Phelps, Dion Boucicault, Fechter, Planché, Doré, Daumier, Gilbert, and a few more.

Doré. As producer, Irving absorbed much from the work of this Frenchman of prolific fancy — a very theatrical fancy — not only a scenical, but a dramatical fancy: Doré was illustrator, and the producer-actor is an illustrator, too. At times, as in the case of Appia and, in a lesser degree, Bakst, the man who designs can be creative — not merely an illustrator: briefly stated, he is not repeating in a drawing something written down by the writer — the creator. Appia and Bakst were not producers, not even stage-managers, but they were in a great degree creators. In the many books which treat of these two, this is not made clear — but their work has had high tribute paid to it.

Doré was not creative, but he was the very devil of an inventor. *Don Quixote* [2] — see how he illustrates the line, "*Don Quixote, thus unhappily hurt, was extremely sullen and melancholy*" (Page 586); this is all Irving: Again, "'*Bless me!*' *she cried,* '*what is this?*'" (Page 587); again all Irving. I don't mean Irving took these designs and did them out again in his acting version of *Don Quixote* — I mean he entered into the very essence of these two designs — absorbed every scrap that was in them — added his own power to them — and there, as he walks across the stage, say, in *Faust,* or comes on in *Louis XI,* there comes friend Doré, helping him. Again, see Page 447, with "*The venerable Montesinos fell on his knees before the afflicted knight*" — a Henry Irving production

[2] The references are to the English edition, Cassell, Petter and Galpin, with text by J. W. Clark, M.A., and notes by Teignmouth Shore, M.A. No date — it was, I suppose, about 1880, though the French edition came out some years earlier.

is in the figures and the whole composition — and the intensity, plus the tranquillity of it is there — again H. I.

Sometimes he would take a whole design of Doré's and put it on the stage — as in the illustration to the line, " *Oh, ye Tobosian wines! that awaken in my mind the thoughts of the sweet pledge of my most bitter sorrow.*" (Page 416.) The wines don't count with H. I. — what struck him was, " deuced good scene for *Romeo and Juliet,* where I come across the a-poth-e-cary " — and, since the scene-painter could invent nothing better, he had it carried out, with a few changes.

The Irving sense returns to you over and over again as you turn each page of Doré's *Quixote,* and feel the curious romanticism — the *curious* romanticism — of every touch. In Doré's *Dante,* it is just as evident. All Doré contains seeds of Irving, and all Irving shows the influence of this excellent inventor. Doré was born in 1833, and so was five years older than Irving.

JOHN GILBERT was another illustrator to whom Irving would turn — but, " not the same inventiveness — what? "

I, who owe a debt to Doré, know quite well what it was H. I. found so excellent. Décors? . . . oh dear, no. Drama expressed visually? — yes.

Now comes another and a greater artist who, I believe, influenced Irving — HONORÉ DAUMIER. But I cannot speak with surety of this, so I will leave it alone. All I know is that Daumier and Irving have things — dramatic things — very much in common. Daumier was born in 1808 and died in 1879.

It was not Daumier, I think, who gave Irving a clue as to how to *look* the last scene of *Louis XI*. I believe it was Doré's influence again. Had Doré seen him — had he come to supper in the Beef Steak Room, had he and Irving been together even once in their lives, I doubt whether either would have been able to help the other more than it happened without meeting. For there is no mention of Doré in Irving records, neither in Brereton's *Life* nor in Bram Stoker's *Personal Reminiscences*.

Seeing CHARLES KEAN's productions probably helped Irving — but it seems to me that what was unique in an Irving production was not at all what he got from Kean — not at all. In *Henry VIII*, in *Richard III*, in *Louis XI*, in *Hamlet*, maybe the Kean notions served — but the Irving inventions were the thing which lighted up these old affairs — I speak with all respect — and these inventions were all clustering around H. I., and kept there — the concentrated essence of the dramatic.

PHELPS. There was once upon a time a very good friend of Irving's, called Mr. Chance Newton. He is an old man now — but he was a lad when he first met Irving, at the Queen's Theatre. He liked acting, and for a while he played some small parts — but his greatest part was that of *Carados*, performed weekly for over fifty years on the stage of the Theatre Democratic, *Referee*.

To Irving he devoted seventy-two pages of his book, *Cues and Curtain Calls*, issued by The Bodley Head, and I have read these pages several times, with great delight. What *Carados* reports about Irving and Phelps is important to us here, though I am positive that Irving exaggerated, as a generous man will do who has received something.

My friend [says Irving to Carados] *you are a lucky fellow! You should render thanksgiving every day that you had the privilege of ten years of Phelps, even though it was his last ten years! I, too, was similarly blessed, but I saw Phelps long before you did—and I saw him play at the 'Wells' a different part every night. Hamlet, one night; King Lear, the next; Timon of Athens the next; Christopher Sly the following night; Sir Giles Overreach the next, and so forth.*

Phelps gave me my 'notice' the first week I was with him [added Irving], *but nevertheless he was the greatest actor I ever saw—or ever shall see. And you and I well know, old friend, that whatever is best in my work at the Lyceum—not only in playing but also in production—you and I both know, d——d well, that is* all *Phelps!*

This " *all* Phelps " is, I would suggest, a fantastic, generous exaggeration.

I daresay he learnt from Phelps how to begin to act — how to stand and deliver speeches — but alas, much as he venerated this great actor, he felt that that wouldn't quite do for him. " Marvellous actor," I imagine him saying — but he meant, " Not in my line at all."

I am of the opinion that he alone was in his line.

From DION BOUCICAULT (1822–1890), I think he derived a good deal. Here was an Irishman of genius — a practical actor-playwright — just as our Pinero is. An Irishman, but of French descent — and one who held the stage for some twenty years. I believe that one of the things taught by Boucicault was the importance of making a theatre pay. He was an experimenter, and so was Irving.

Then FECHTER — other actors in London poo-pooed Fechter — not so H. I. Irving was watching him very carefully — cutting him up as he did Doré — " no good, that sort of thing, but this . . ." and he takes a leaf out of *his* book. Fechter (born about 1823, died in 1888), was in England, and playing in London, from 1860 to 1869, during which time he played *The Corsican Brothers, Hamlet, Othello, Robert Macaire* (1865), *Claude Melnotte* (in *The Lady of Lyons*), and *Monte Cristo* — being for four years manager of the Lyceum (1863-1867). Irving was then still Brodribb, remember.

What of ROBSON? I'm puzzled here — but at a venture I'd wager with a fair amount of confidence that he was of use to Irving.

PLANCHÉ (1796-1880), doubtless helped Irving — as he helped every producer. "*Planché*," writes R. W. Lowe in 1888, "*exerted a great influence for good on the theatrical world of his time,*" through Charles Kemble, Madame Vestris, Charles Kean, and many more.

In 1867, Irving (still Brodribb), went over to Paris — acted with an English company (it was no success) and H. I. lingered behind till the end of the month. No more is said. I have tried to discover exactly what was being played in all the theatres during the last part of the month of July 1867. Bancroft says he stayed two months: but one week — three days, even, is time enough for an Irving to learn what another will not learn in three years.

All I can discover is that the new opera house by Garnier was being put up, and that Gounod's *Roméo et*

Juliette was played for the first time in 1867, April 27th, at the Théâtre Lyrique; and that isn't much. What I wanted to discover was whether the *mélodrame,* the *Courrier de Lyon,* with Paulin Ménier acting in it, was still in the repertoire of its theatre, the Gaîté I believe. It was first produced on March 16, 1850, and Paulin Ménier played not *Dubosc,* but *Chopard* — the second villain of the piece — and Ménier made it an unforgettable performance: " *like an appallingly grotesque apparition,*" Georges Cain writes of it, and asks:

Who, having seen him, did not retain the terrifying memory of that mastiff's head; those eyes of a beast of prey, gleaming under the thick tuft of the brows; that chin, deep in the folds of a dirty cravat; that toothless mouth; that red nose; those short whiskers on the purple cheeks; the little opera-hat pushed down on the simian skull; the hussar's waistcoat, which must once have been red, and from which a few brass buttons still hung; the extraordinary coat with its lapels; the short-handled hunting-crop; the shabby boots; the leather breeches, striped with darns and seams — and above all, the astonishing voice which proceeded from this uncanny figure — a voice which was hoarse, debauched, drunken, uttering its unforgettable: " Ici, Fouinard! "

And did Irving catch a glimpse of Frédéric Lemaître — also playing astonishing *mélodrame* in Paris at that epoch?

These may or may not have served him well, but one master who without doubt served him as he has done a hundred others, was CHARLES DICKENS. Some there are who cannot read Charles Dickens — there are times when one cannot read the Bible, or Osbert Sitwell — at other times both of these are delightful, both of them profound. It does depend — does it not — on our mood. I have read Du Boisgoby in a fiendish translation, and found him profound — technically of immense interest — important. At other times, even in the same day, I have said, "What infernal rubbish" — but I have had to add "and yet —."

It's the bones of drama and the dramatic romance in things, books and all, which I cannot resist — and so when Mr. Micawber stalks out and says something from the book called *David Copperfield,* how wonderful it seems — how wonderful it is. And all Dickens was especially wonderful to Irving: and when he is *Dubosc* he is Dickens, and when he is *Lesurques* he is Dickens. He is guided by Dickens in *Richard III* and in *Charles the First,* as well as in *Eugene Aram* and *Robert Landry.*

Only in *The Bells* is he all Irving — though Dickens, Daumier, Boucicault, Kean (Edmund), may be hanging around somewhere in the wings. Doré is then only in a stall, and watching enwrapt.

These, then, were some of Irving's influences. Add to them the name of E. W. Godwin, whose influence was all over the production of *The Cup,* although it may not be known — and we see how little, after all, Irving was influenced. He helped himself, having no school, to choose his own tutors. It is what every wise man does, only some are more apt than others as pupils.

IRVING AS THEATRE DIRECTOR

AND NOW the story takes a turn — can we today awaken very much excitement on hearing of actor management, and of the leaders of the stage? And yet it is curious that we more often hear and read of Irving the actor manager, of Irving the leader of the English stage, and even of Irving the courteous host, than we do of Irving the actor. Great stress is laid upon these three rôles of his — all three are considered " important." Is it, I wonder sometimes, because they are connected with money? The lavish actor manager — the generous host — really the whole thing has been overdone.

The story of Irving the actor manager has been told in detail by Austin Brereton. The book, which seems to me to be an excellent one in many ways, was published in 1908, and consists of some seven hundred pages, wherein most of the facts have been very correctly put down, and any amount of figures given. These figures are interesting, because they show quite clearly that, given an artist, a great play can be just as much of a success as a little play.

The manager is, after all, only the assistant of the actor, when they are two different men, or when the two are combined in one man. It is, in the final estimate, an annoyance to any actor to have to assume the cares of management, and it was an annoyance to Irving. But managers are curiously unable to understand their job; and so, were Irving alive today, he would still be forced to become an actor-manager, because presumably he would be unable to find a single man in London who could assist him in the proper manner. He could find one or two showmen, who would want to run him while running a variety show and some other attractions at the same time — the Augustus Harrises of the day — but no man serious enough to realize that in every period there is always one artist for whom it's worth while scrapping the side-shows.

Why should it be so difficult to assist — to save an artist infinite trouble — to save him from wearing out his life — why should it be so difficult? It is only difficult when theatre-managers and showmen are so conceited. If you will inquire in London today, you will find no manager for Henry Irving, because you will, after a very long inquiry, discover an amazing fact; and it is this — the managers think they *are* Henry Irvings. They believe themselves to be artists. This is one of the oddest phases that the theatrical profession in England has for some time experienced, for such conceit is of a very obstinate character. Smugness will do anything rather than drop its smirk. Theoretically it is wrong for an actor to be his own manager, but if tomorrow London is over-run by actor managers, and you begin to complain, you will have no one but yourselves to blame, for the actor has put up too long with the antics of the showman who is not an artist, who believes he is, and who is out of his place today.

An old actor of the eighteenth century and the early nineteenth, was indifferent as to who managed the theatre or who managed the stage, so long as everyone kept out of his way when he was on the boards, and fed him properly with his cues.

An old actor's care was to represent the character of *Richard III* or *Othello,* not to interpret the plays: to get through the part and receive an ovation and a cheque — not a report of the night's receipts, nor a bill of the week's expenses. The old actor yearned for no unnecessary responsibility — he did not like being harassed. To be annoyed by having to think of his companions' efforts — of their lack of talent — of their insufferable pretensions — this would be found to harass him, and so he would have nothing to do with selecting a cast, rehearsing the troupe, arranging the sceneries, or timing the curtains. He looked to a hack to do this. That hack was called *stage-manager.*

The old actor did not like to be troubled as to how to balance accounts — how to run a theatre — or how to get the public into the theatre. It would have overwhelmed him had he been asked to draw up a programme. So long as he figured as the one important feature of that programme, nothing else mattered; and he looked to another hack — a rather superior hack — to prepare it, to make the audience comfortable, to work up the business, to attend to the front of the house. This rather superior hack was called the *showman* or *business-manager.* He was also called the *acting-manager,* but the title had no reference to the craft of acting on a stage — it meant a manager who acted for the company of performers in all matters of business.

So much for the old actor of more than a hundred years ago. But another kind of actor came along. Leading actors (Charles Kean, for example) ceased to be indifferent as to how the stage and the stalls were managed: they assumed the responsibilities of these two extra jobs, and thus became actor managers. They managed the whole theatre — the front of the house and the stage — and they managed it in their own interest. Some found it profitable, and some found it ruinous.

It exercised an actor's capacity for affairs; his sound common sense (if he had any) was exercised; his time was full of interesting things to see to. He felt that a responsibility which was carried on after he had done his own part was rather enjoyable, and even helpful to him — left him fewer idle hours, kept him in good health — he felt a good deal less bored — and so it came about that many of the better actors, and certainly the better types of men, became actor managers.

The actor manager was head of his own house and family (that is to say, theatre and company) — and that was all very much to the good.

After it became *a system* — when every actor took the habit — it was all to the bad, and then it fell to pieces.

I will not stop here to tell over again why as a system that of actor manager is a very bad one — I am only happy here in telling what a very good thing it was for us all that Irving became an actor manager.

As a manager he behaved like one, and as a rule controlled any rash but idealistic tendencies of that actor whom he was serving — his other self.

That actor, being excessively fond of play-acting, would naturally be everlastingly wanting to skip from play to play. His idea would be to act a different part night after night. Experience had taught Irving that to do this was to do what was most pleasant, not only for himself but for other actors. He was also sure that this way — this repertory way — was the best for the art of the Theatre, as it was called. He stood in no need of any prompting about this matter — the experience of twenty-three years had shown him, by the year 1879, when he became manager of the Lyceum, that the old repertory system was the right one — and yet he decided against it . . . why?

The answer is this — that Irving the actor very wisely left the decision in this matter in the hands of Irving the manager. Manager Irving was not going to risk any chance of failure. Although he appreciated the many suggestions which rained in on him, as to how to run the Lyceum, he decided to run it like a sensible Englishman, on sound business lines.

This did not mean to him that it was necessary to run the place exactly like a shop — but it meant this, that so long as there were people who were ready to fill the Lyceum Theatre to see his first production, he would show it to them, and not turn to a second one.[1]

He did this because London had grown so considerably since the days of Macready, and was entirely altered since

---

[1] I do not wish to suggest that Irving would have run any piece as pieces are run today — for a year or longer — or farm out different versions so as to coin money. He was positively not that sort of showman.

those of Garrick. Macready had not been able to do all he wanted to do — his Diary shows you that he longed for more time and for longer runs. People on the stage were by that time saying that it would be more satisfactory if they had a few more weeks in which to prepare a production, so as to somewhat perfect it. With Irving, this soon became a conviction. He detested vamping a thing — he was very British in that. Either a thing was worth doing very well, worth spending time and money on, or it was not worth doing at all. Irving felt this no less because the thing he wished to do was something people wished to pay to see. When the question of people paying him came into his mind, it settled that mind once and for all — and decided him to give them what he could in full measure. Irving as manager was therefore not merely acting as a sensible Englishman, but as a very honourable idealist. He would give all he could give to a public that was generously paying into his box office all he asked from it.

When folk some day shall be critical about the managers of the nineteenth century for having smashed up the old repertory system, let them remember what I have said, and attribute to a few of them, and especially Irving, better motives than they have been able to find up to now.

BESIDES all this, Irving as a manager was able to show the actor Irving, that there was an advantage to him in having a long run — provided he was a careful actor. The advantage lay in achieving a certain perfection — a finish. The careless actor may say, "Night after night I have to utter the same lines, and hear the same lines repeated by the others, and it wearies me ": but the wise actor will say (provided the play is a good one), " I am enabled, by these long runs, to perfect my part: to correct on Tuesday what I found wrong on Monday: being actor manager I am even enabled to arrange a scene differently, or change an actor and substitute another for him — so that during the season the performance of the whole piece is slowly improving. We can do as a clever gardener does, who snips away the dead and dying blossoms, so that his garden appears always in a state of perfection."

These few simple notions had not occurred to Richard Monckton Milnes, first Baron Houghton, when, on the evening of the 14th of February 1880, as one of Irving's guests at a banquet to celebrate the 100th night of a play, he made a thoughtless speech, saying that long runs of plays were not beneficial to art.

Had an artist made the statement, as an artist amongst artists, it would have been one thing; but for any member of Queen Victoria's House of Lords to be so tactless as to forget that almost every other country in the world possessed a National Theatre, provided for by the State, and that it was only to such State Theatres, not to a single artist, that one could look to spend millions in upholding an art — even the Dramatic art — to forget this was not a little dull.

CHARLES KEAN, Charles Mathews, and Macready had been actor managers before Irving — and I fancy that Charles Kean was one of the very best of men to fill this special calling. But Charles Kean would seem to have been less actor than manager, and should have been called a manager-actor. Irving was essentially actor — actor all over — in and out, so that the more you pull him to pieces, the more the actor comes into evidence.

I have said this so often that you will begin to be offended, till you realize that it is not for you I drum it out, but for those who are rather hard of hearing.

And he knew himself, and he could say to himself: "Mr. Chatterton, of Drury Lane Theatre, finds that Shakespeare spells ruin, because, poor fellow, now that I have left him, he has no one to play Shakespeare. *I* can play Shakespeare. I can also play the easy part of Frederick Balzir Chatterton, and with rather more determination, and considerably more know-ledge."

I daresay that he said a good deal more about this celebrated but stupid theatrical manager of Drury Lane: I say "stupid" because Chatterton *had Irving in his company for nearly a year,* 1869, *and failed to recognize his genius.* Ten years later Chatterton was bankrupt, but he had anyhow invented that infamous saying, "Shakespeare spells ruin." Shakespeare ruined Chatterton and rewarded Irving.

Unless Irving had become an actor manager, we should never have seen Shakespeare's plays given as Irving gave them to us. Some there are who have criticized Irving: it was because they hated him, and that's all there is about it. They attacked him for not acting like Barry Sullivan or Salvini — though he was Irving, they objected that he should act like Irving, and be always Irving. How comic of them, for Chopin is always Chopin, no matter what he writes — even as Rachel and Bernhardt were Rachel and Bernhardt. Have you ever heard anyone who objected to Chopin, Rachel, Bernhardt, being themselves? Well then!

And they attacked Irving for surrounding himself with a third-rate company of actors, unmindful of the fact — surely not unaware of it — that his company included some of the best actors in England. And had he selected a company of what critics always describe so incorrectly as inferior men, it would have been but following a cautious tradition. Boaden, in his *Life of Mrs. Jordan*, tells us that *" to have great names for trivial business is certain death to any author. The spectators soon see that the performers are discontented in their situations."* [2] It was not customary to have star actors playing the rôles of *Lorenzo, Gratiano, Old Gobbo,* the *Duke,* and so forth; and in melodramas such as Irving so often produced, it would have been useless to engage Mr. Herbert Beerbohm Tree, Mr. Charles Wyndham, Mr. Hare, and half-a-dozen more, to play the minor rôles.

It is ridiculous of these people to attempt to find fault with such an achievement as Irving's, in which the aim was spirited and the method practical. He knew what it was he wanted, and that what he wanted was best, and he abided faithfully by that; and it was for this that he was continually being abused by whipper-snappers — *chicker-leary coves* was, I think, at that time the precise term. The real motive behind these attacks was not at first clear to

---

[2] The copy of this book in my possession belonged to my mother, and I note that she has marked this passage.

anyone, but pretty soon it became clear: Irving had refused to act one of their plays. What is more, he had even gone so far as to dam the torrent of their eloquence, which eloquence resolved itself into: " You're a fool. I can manage you, your theatre, your leading lady, your box office and all a hundred times better than you — now listen to me."

Irving, with all the good will in the world, patient even to a fault, really had no time to listen to these gentlemen who suffered under the delusion that they could annex the Lyceum Theatre for their own curiously impudent little purposes.

Irving had to go on. It was perhaps but natural that one of these ambitious ones of the period should see in the Lyceum Theatre a ready-made playbox to his hand — but it was not very intelligent of him, and it was excessively ill mannered.

Irving was the perfection of good manners — grace itself — never pitched his voice up cockily — always stopped to listen — to consider any suggestion — was always ready to say " I do not know."

And his chief reason for this was that he was determined to act the part of manager well, although a very dull part; and he acted it so well for a number of years, that he automatically became the leader of the English stage.

IRVING AS LEADER OF THE
ENGLISH STAGE

LEADER of the English stage, Irving was also head of the profession — two different things. Stanislavsky is leader of the Russian stage, but is hardly head of its profession, as Reinhardt is head of the German profession, for Stanislavsky is concerned very little with the Theatre as a money-making affair: and as we know, a man may lead the State, and yet not be head of the Government. Garibaldi undoubtedly led Italy, but was a free-lance. Rossetti and Whistler were leaders of the art of painting in England for a time, but neither was President of the Royal Academy. In music, Bach was the leader — and still is — but he never bothered to become head of any society or committee or profession.

But Irving was both.

As leader of the English stage — a very responsible position — Irving had to be doubly careful; careful first of all not to wreck the Lyceum Theatre and, secondly, in no way to assist towards undoing the nation. *To make sure this was so*

At that time it was felt that if you produced a play by Ibsen you had got your knife into poor old England, because, it was said, Ibsen dealt in things not often touched on in England, and dealt in them squalidly — in a cold, damp way — so it was said. I have had moments of emancipation when I felt that there was nobody so splendid as Ibsen — until I emancipated myself still further, and discovered that Shakespeare beat him hollow on his own ground — and that there was still another land or two further south — and a civilization or two further east.

Shakespeare is still the most advanced English thinker and writer of the day; and there are times when I seriously feel that a special Commission ought to be set up — and without delay — to inquire into the plays written by this man, and to see whether it would not be possible to substitute those of some safer dramatist — plays which everyone would admit are plain, harmless, and easily digestible food, in place of this strange and terrible Shakespeare.

Now it is astonishing to think that it is this awful creature, Shakespeare, with his horrible, if at times beautiful visions, which the responsible head of the dramatic profession in the Victorian era sponsored for some ten to fifteen years: and it is a still more solemn thought to realize that the entire nation loved it — and our venerable and dear Queen quite approved.

Besides these plays by Shakespeare, Irving produced plays translated from the French, and also some of the plays of Sheridan, Lord Tennyson, and Lord Byron, with indifferent fortune — although Tennyson's *Becket* was received with delight on account of Irving's own performance.

But there were two writers whose plays he did not touch: these were, Augustin Eugène Scribe and George Bernard Shaw.

I have put them together, for they are a pair. We can accept the verdict of the majority, and not Irving's verdict, in this case. Each writer was very clever. Each went in for writing plays — unreal, of an artificiality which belongs to the special times in which each lived — nothing worse. As fashion-plates, this pair will not prove useless to those future historians of the times and of the stage — but the labour of these same historians will perforce be long and tedious: for the amount written about Monsieur Scribe and about Mr. Shaw is stupendous; indefatigable workers have a talent for making the world scribble about them — and A. E. S. and G. B. S. were indefatigable, splendid workers . . . the man who built the Pyramids [1] laboured less.

In one year alone — in 1821 — Scribe wrote and saw acted fourteen of his *comédie-vaudevilles . . . four-teen ! ! !*

Between 1820 and 1830 he wrote for the Gymnase over one hundred plays. In 1830–31, sixteen of his plays were produced. Most of them made money.

All over Europe, too — something to the same extent as G. B. S. is making money all over Europe . . . the man who built the Pyramids made less.

I have a suspicion that no one really *likes* the work of either A. E. S. or G. B. S. — I have the feeling that no one possibly could do so — but, and this is an important point, which the astute side of Irving actually failed to perceive — the plays of both of them have paid well.

Put on a play by Mr. Bernard Shaw, and it will run awhile, and pay: so was it with M. Eugène Scribe: and

---

[1] William Blake has drawn his portrait, and this is often reproduced. See *Life of William Blake,* by Gilchrist (Lane, 1907, face page 270).

this argument, with essentially sensible men, is such a powerful argument. Irving was not sensible like that — you could not buy him.

In Berlin, Stockholm, Milan, Zurich, Budapest, Vienna, Rome, and Barcelona; in many provincial towns of England, and in most of the cities in America — in all these places you will find a play by Mr. Shaw being performed this very month. Did Marie Corelli ever achieve such popularity — does Mr. Edgar Wallace sell quite so well as this?

It was the same with Scribe — he was here, there, everywhere, all over the shop.

Why, then, did Irving, reputed to be a man with some talent for spotting a winner, and not disdainful of success — why did he reject both Scribe and Shaw?

The two writers were very different men — one with a passionate brain, the other unmoved up there — but each had the facilities in that direction where most useful. Each could reel it off — could put it over — and neither was at all backward in haggling for the spoils of war. The gift of the gab, the slick capacity to write apace without bothering about anything further — alike as two pins — Monsieur Scribe, the matter-of-fact little democrat, is unacted today, and may soon be forgotten. Mr. Shaw, " the concierge in the house of literature," is acted today.

I wonder what instinct warned Henry Irving to keep away from Scribe and Shaw?

How is it that a melodrama, *The Bells,* by Leopold Lewis, is so much better than a good play by Mr. Bernard Shaw;

Walker's exhibition, the Eidouranian. March 21, 1817.

for, as everyone begins to realize, Mr. Shaw writes a play
moderately well.

I must bore you and explain what a melodrama is —
and how it was of use to Irving: bear with me a little, I
beg of you.

A melodrama is a pure product of the Theatre: every
great play has in it the best elements of melodrama —
witness *Macbeth, Othello,* and *Hamlet.*

Melodrama was invented about 1600 by Italians, and
they called it *Drama in musica.* It has since then branched
off into two divisions, *Opera* and *Mélodrame.* A fable
was taken and retold in verse: recitative was employed —
chorus in song and in dance. The music was sometimes
incidental, and sometimes of a purely dramatic character,
as it still was in 1870 in the French *mélodrame.* Altogether a delight — not an accursed sermon in jam like a
Shaw play.

The Beggar's Opera can be called a melodrama. Melodrama was not and is not afraid of the spectacular or the
heroic, of *bravura,* or of the impossible. It shuns one thing
purposely — the matter-of-fact. And a good play by Mr.
Shaw embraces all that is matter-of-fact.

The Bells is a better play than any of Shaw's, for the
reason that it is made of the elements of melodrama, and
has no mission. In a good melodrama the chief character
is kept on the stage most of the time. He is given situations which lend themselves to every able actor to develop.
In developing these to suit his own personality, and to
illumine the plot, he reveals his talent or his genius.

We may approve or disapprove the custom of writing

plays for specially gifted performers — it is too old a custom for a playwright to run counter to. A playwright well practised in his craft will invent such a plot and such situations and such a character for the leading actor or actress, that nothing remains but for the leading actor or actress (also well practised in the craft) to take up the script and fill in the *business,* and let slip the dogs of dramatic wrath.

Mr. Shaw, for some unknown reason, selected to do more than a practised playwright does. This " more " consisted in adding to his text a number of stage-directions of great length, explaining what each character was to do.[2]

Such a play he took to Irving in 1896. It was called *The Man of Destiny*. Irving rejected the play — it was, after all, only a curtain-raiser — and he rejected it because, by putting in all the stage-directions (most of them taken from things he had seen Irving do), Shaw positively bored Irving — as was to be expected.

A dramatist, if he particularly wish to, may show off in his text as much as he please — as a dramatist. To attempt to show off in the stage-directions, as a performer, is unwise. Suburbia's wife thinks it's awfully clever of the dear man, but no one else does. To overload his play with stage-directions for the producer, the actor, and the actress, is tactless. They have their craft at their finger-ends, and they will hardly need any schooling from the dramatist. Such schooling is apt to offend them — it does offend them; for we must remember that they too, after ten or twelve years' practice, have ideas of how to interpret a rôle

[1] He has done this in all his plays.

or how to use the stage, since that is their job; and no one
knows it as well as they do. From Shakespeare to Sir
Arthur Pinero, good dramatists who have been actors have
recognized this.

But if to write down in the text what the usual run of
actors are to do, and how they are to look, be at all discourteous, it is more than discourteous — it is ridiculous —
to write down in the text what an exceptional actor of
genius is to do, and *to write down things that the dramatist
has seen this very actor do in several plays.* These inventions of the actor are *his* inventions, and to lift them from
Irving's portrayal of *Iago,* from *Richelieu,* from *Philip,*
and a dozen other parts, as Mr. Shaw has done, and to slap
them into the manuscript and send such a manuscript to
Irving, was a blunder.

Turn to this play, *The Man of Destiny,* and see for
yourself where these tactless superfluities occur.

My references are to the 1914 edition issued by Constable
& Co.

In the first two pages of the five-page explanation of
who Buonaparte is, what like, and what the scene is like,
Mr. Shaw contradicts himself, stating that the French
Commander is twenty-seven years old and also twenty-
six. Irving was more exact than this.

Mr. Shaw then begins to instruct the producer, Irving,
how to be very original in the way he is to open the scene.
He describes in crisp, Shawish sentences, a stage picture
such as we were given by the Bancrofts or Mr. John Hare,
or by the elder Boucicault, in 1870–1880, and as built and
painted by Mr. Hawes Craven, Mr. Telbin, dozens of

times. And Mr. Shaw had seen the kind of thing at the Lyceum too — in *The Bells,* or in *The Lyons Mail*. Interior parlour of old Inn: Italy — a hundred engravings to help the producer — up-stage centre, the big door and windows, with vineyard and courtyard as backing — on the left, big sideboard covered with dishes and plates for dinner — on the right, fireplace, with couch near it — right upper entrance, another door, leading to an inner room. Centre of stage, a table covered with usual stage props for meal. The Landlord. Napoleon discovered at table, working and eating at the same time. He is correcting a map, "*and occasionally marks the position of the forces by taking a grape skin from his mouth and planting it on the map with his thumb, like a wafer.*" I quote the two lines in full, for here we come to not a Hare, Boucicault, or Bancroft touch, but to some pseudo-Irving. As it is precisely the sort of thing Irving did, it was not a little boorish of G. B. S. to ape the actor in this mannerless way.

So satisfied is G. B. S. with this achievement, that he immediately follows it up by a howler. "*He* (Buonaparte) *has a supply of writing materials before him, mixed up in disorder with the dishes and cruets: and his long hair gets sometimes into the risotto gravy and sometimes into the ink.*"

He is unaware that even the low-comedy actor of but little standing would reject anything so cheap, and yet supposes that the grim Irving will delight in this delicate touch with the hair in the gravy.

A few lines further on, we find, "*Buonaparte marks the map with gravy, using his fork as a pen.*"

It is a wonder that he does not increase the subtlety of this horse-play by explaining that the gravy is so hot that *"Buonaparte puts his finger in the gravy, and jumps."* That at least would have been seen by the audience, and might get a laugh from the front row of the stalls — whereas what has gone before would not even have been noted.

The Landlord is now ordered by the author to clear the table in the approved fashion of the London stage in 1875, chattering as he does it. Ever fresh, but 1875 for all that, and the author thoroughly convinced that he is teaching Irving " how to do it." Jolly nice, this old theatrical business of landlords and tables to clear, and patter all the time. I could watch and listen to it for ever, but I never go so far as to suppose I invented it — it's as old as the hills, and as dusty. Only now and again an actor of genius can make it appear as fresh as a bed of violets.

This reliance on actors of talent, on men like Alfred Bishop, Arliss, Wassmann and Artem, leads all good dramatists to write down a brief *" clears table "* — but leads Mr. Bernard Shaw to insult them by writing down the following:

As he chatters he takes the cloth off without removing the map and inkstand, and takes the corners in his hands and the middle in his mouth to fold it up . . . he folds and rolls up the cloth, emphasising his phrases by the steps of the process . . . fold . . . fold . . . at the last fold he slaps the cloth on the table and deftly rolls it up, adding by way of peroration " Conquer one: conquer all." *He takes the cloth to the sideboard and puts it in the drawer.*

Mr. Shaw, having seen the Barry Sullivan type of actor swallow the cloth and get a round of applause, naturally wishes to prevent anything quite so theatrical, and advises the actor to do what every actor except Barry Sullivan would do, did do, and always will do.

Anon comes the lady of the piece — the lady, it was intended by Mr. Shaw, should be played by Miss Ellen Terry. No sooner does he think of this character than he thinks out something *very* clever for her to do. Ellen Terry, whom he admires, whose genius he cannot over-praise, Ellen Terry must be taught what to do. She must not be spontaneous, as Irving always loved her to be; no, she must do clever things à la Shaw. Therefore this is put down:

A lady's voice (*calling from some distant part of the inn*) "Giuseppe!" (*The voice is very musical, and the two final notes make an ascending interval.*)

You see, Shaw felt there was a real danger here — there was the risk that Ellen Terry, spite of her genius and some thirty years' experience on the English stage, might call out "*Giū — seppe*" — unmusically, and with the accent on the "*Giu*" — a snappy "*seppe*" following on.

After this we have one or two more of these Arliss-Bishop suggestions as to how the Landlord is to do his every bit, and how Irving is to accompany him; how Irving is to speak "*absently*," and when he is to speak as though "*startled*." It's touching, this nurse-like attention lest the little ones slip.

Ellen Terry's next remark — still off-stage — is to be
rather different from the preceding one: here we have it:

The Lady's voice (*the two final notes now making a per-
emptory descending interval*) "Giuseppe."

Ellen Terry's third remark is to be once more " *Giuseppe*" — this time " (*impatiently*)."

You see, the author — Mr. Bernard Shaw — is never
quite certain whether the contemptible actor, Irving,
and that genius of an actress, Ellen Terry, are going to
do the thing properly: this is why, when a word has
to be said " *sympathetically*," or " *absently*," or
" *brusquely*," he writes it all down. Then he feels sure
that his play will be properly acted by these two puppets of his, in the safe, old-fashioned way which he
adores.

And so the stage-directions go on and on, all taken from
performances seen by Mr. Shaw in the seventies and
eighties.

At last we reach the entrance of the *Strange Lady* — the
Ellen Terry part which Ellen Terry never played.

He takes a page and a quarter to describe the entrance,
when three lines would have sufficed Sir Arthur Pinero,
and three words — " *enter Strange Lady* " — would have
sufficed Shakespeare. He describes Ellen Terry's face,
figure, and general appearance in the many parts he had
seen her in. He puts down what she is to do: it is probably
what the real Ellen Terry would *not* have done, but it's
the obvious thing an ordinary G. B. S. Ellen Terry would
do. At last he comes to this:

The next moment a wave of colour rushes up from beneath the creamy fichu and drowns her whole face. One can see that she is blushing all over her body.

This little touch, vulgarly expressed, is another filching from the stage, not a gift to it — for in June 1895, he had been to see Eleonora Duse play the part of *Magda* at Drury Lane Theatre, and had there seen her do her famous blush in the third act. Mr. Shaw described this blushing in the *Saturday Review* the same week. The passage is to be found in his *Dramatic Opinions and Essays*. And now, between July and November of that year, when he is writing this play, or touching it up, he puts down what he remembers was so effective in Duse, as a little notion of his own.

This is immediately followed by a few more lines of 1875 stage-directions, in which he tells the actor of the part of the young lieutenant what *he* has to do. The young lieutenant "*then seizing her by the wrist, pulls her past him into the room as he claps the door to, and plants himself with his back to it.*" Haven't we seen it done? — over and over again! It's the old, ordinary 1875 way again. And this is the suggestion of a man who wanted to teach Irving his business — who wanted to bring Irving flush with the coming twentieth century.

I recall that when I produced Ibsen's *Vikings at Helgoland,* for my mother, at the Imperial Theatre in 1903, Mr. Shaw, inexact as usual, wrote to her to the effect that I had distorted the whole opening scene: that the sun should have been shining brightly at the beginning, and that "into this sunlit scene stalks Hiordis, a figure of gloom."

Alas! I had done a foolish thing — I had followed the directions of a playwriter: Ibsen distinctly states in his first five lines, that "*it is a stormy, snow-grey winter day.*" This is what I gave: I made it rather darker than I should have done with more experience, but it was a stormy winter day, right enough. In Helgoland, the sky on a stormy winter day is lead-colour. Where the "sunlit scene" comes in is later on, after, not before Hiordis's entrance. Ibsen writes "*The storm has meanwhile ceased; the midday sun is now visible like a red disc, low upon the rim of the sea*" — and there I put it. After all, Mr. Shaw but reflected the opinion of a certain Anna Blunden Martino, who signed herself, in a letter to me, "*Old enough to be your grandmother.*" She, too, wrote to me about the "sunburnt men" she had hoped to see, and failed to observe what it was that Ibsen had quite definitely described. A theatre-manager in the provinces once objected to a poster for *Hamlet,* by the Beggarstaffs, being all black and grey — he said he wanted it in colour . . . !!

One should, I feel, attend to what Shakespeare and Ibsen are saying — rather than to the brighter suggestions so delicately advanced by Mr. Bernard Shaw or Mrs. Anna Blunden Martino. Irving thought so, at any rate.

IRVING AS HOST

THE COURTEOUS old British public which assembled at the Lyceum Theatre was the enthusiastic public of the Victorian era, and to delight this public Irving spared himself no pains. Today, the old British public is not so well considered: it has been done out of its theatres, for it has no theatres to go to as in those days, so it splits itself up and exercises its courtesy by veiling its enthusiasm. It pops into all the show places — it cares for no one place in particular.

In those days, in 1881, we had seven such places — at least seven real permanent playhouses. *Drury Lane Theatre* for spectacular drama, under Augustus Harris; the *Adelphi Theatre* for light melodrama and farce, under the Gattis; the *Savoy* for light opera, under D'Oyle Carte; the *Haymarket* for light comedy, under Bancroft and later under Tree; the *Surrey* for the very heaviest of melodrama, under Conquest; the *St. James's* for domestic drama, under Kendall; and the *Lyceum* for tragedy, classic, and comedy, under Irving.

We had about thirty-three other theatres, but these seven were so much the *homes* of their special genus of drama, that Londoners never had to trouble to think which theatre they would go to, for they knew that these seven theatres could be relied on not to chop and change. To say, " Let's go to the Adelphi," meant the certainty of seeing a stunning popular melodrama, written by a skilled hand (one who always wrote for that playhouse), and acted by Henry Neville or William Terriss, in a dashing way — not Irving's way, but the old T. P. Cooke way.

The public was considered and helped by this system: people would never be disappointed, never worried to death lest, on getting to the *Adelphi*, they might discover there some Continental or American company, acting something excellently well, but something they didn't want to see: the public had its mind made up about what it wanted to see, and it did not allow itself to be put off.

"Let us go to the *Savoy*," meant, let us go and hear Gilbert and Sullivan — see and listen to George Grossmith (the elder) and the picked company which D'Oyle Carte had assembled and kept together, so that we, the public, might rely on him to interpret for us one masterpiece after another — *The Gondoliers, The Mikado, Pinafore, Iolanthe, Ruddigore.*

In this way the theatre-goer could be sure that every one of his evenings would be a success. London was large then — it seemed so to us — it's no smaller today — so we liked to plan an evening's entertainment by fixing a place to go to, and we liked to be sure to find our actors in their places — better, we felt, than to find them out of place.

In Irving's time there were also seven music halls on which another public could rely. "Come along to the *Tivoli*," we said, just as we said "What about the *Lyceum*?" sure every time of what we were to see — something first-rate — and sure of the pleasant, familiar house itself into which we were going.

It's nice to be at home — and we were at home at the seven theatres and seven music halls. We were made to feel at home: the personal appearance of the director or business manager helped things: if the director was the artist (as at the Lyceum), then it was necessary for someone else to represent him like Mr. Bram Stoker or Mr. Frederick Harrison, who represented Mr. Beerbohm Tree at the Haymarket.

These representatives of the artists were always present at the opening of the doors; they were known figures, always found standing in the entrance-hall, welcoming into the house on their arrival the hundreds of well-known faces, just as we welcome to our own private houses the guests who come to our parties. Very, very important — and a loss of at least £5000 per theatre, now that the custom is forgotten. All over the earth this courtesy is shown by a host in his own house, and this custom should be preserved in our theatres, if we wish to restore them to their old supremacy. We all like to be *made welcome;* no matter where we go, we appreciate the personal greeting, whether it be as we enter a big shop or a church. In the large stores we get that personal attention — yet it has been less evident than it should be, recently, in our theatres.

ON SEPTEMBER 28, 1889, the doors of the Lyceum Theatre opened at 7:30 for the first performance of *The Dead Heart*. Mr. Bram Stoker would be at his post, ready to receive the first comers. Every seat would have been allotted weeks beforehand — he would know where everyone was to be placed. He would recognize all the guests

— and most of the stalls and dress circle seats on an Irving first night were reserved for guests, a courtesy which possibly survives into these days — I have not been at any first night of late years. Coming into the theatre on this first night, Mr. Stoker would see, maybe, Mr. and Mrs. George Lewis, Sir Morel and Lady Mackenzie, Alfred Gilbert, Sir Alexander Mackenzie, Mr. and Mrs. Jopling, Mr. and Mrs. Linley Sambourne, the Tadema family, John Sargent, Max Beerbohm with Aubrey Beardsley, the Duke of Beaufort, William Rothenstein, and the family of Dr. Pryde. A while later, as the clock pointed to five minutes to eight, Sir Edwin Arnold, the Duchess of Teck, Pinero, Labouchere, would arrive: then Lord Londesborough, George Du Maurier and his lovely family, and Dr. and Mrs. Todhunter. Some would drive up in carriages, some in hansoms, some in four-wheelers — others would arrive on foot. In they poured — Mr. and Mrs. Felix Moscheles, the Seligmanns, Mr. and Mrs. Comyns Carr, Lockwood, Walter Gilbey, Edmund Yates, Walter Palmer, Walter Dowdeswell, Mr. and Mrs. Perugini, Mrs. Bancroft, Mr. and Mrs. Walter Pollock . . . dozens of families known to Irving or to Ellen Terry, and all welcomed there by the very able Bram Stoker.

But then this too was a man of character, this Irishman, who as a young student at Trinity College, Dublin, had seen and appreciated the great Barry Sullivan — appreciated him enough to be jealous when Irving came to the capital of Ireland — jealous lest the new-comer should overthrow his friend and countryman, Sullivan — as he did.

But Stoker was a man of feeling, of understanding, and of integrity. He could tell chalk from cheese, and was too real a being — a good Irish being — to care to argue against the angels. Seeing that Irving was a man of the highest genius, he did not make himself ridiculous by upholding Barry Sullivan as something better, for he could see at a glance that nothing was or could be better than Irving.

It was this able and delightful assistant who performed the part of deputy host on a first night, for Irving, until the curtain was lowered at the end of the evening. The general public then went off to their houses, but some few hundred of the invited friends would stay lingering in their places or in the corridors until a new scene was set upon the boards. Then the small door between auditorium and stage would be opened, and everyone would drift through it, and discover long tables laden with good things from Gunters — a cold supper to be eaten standing up.

And amongst his friends came Irving, possibly in evening dress, maybe in his stage costume — it depended, I think, on how much time he had to change in — and for an hour or longer, everyone enjoyed themselves. A few of the players of the evening were invited to be present.

THE Lyceum Theatre of today is physically not the same Lyceum as in 1889. In the Lyceum Theatre today you will not find the old familiar places — the pit and its entrance — the gallery — the old foyers — the boxes — the stalls — are all quite changed. And behind the curtain all is wrecked. The old stage door, and through into the long passage leading to the stage — the two Green Rooms — the third, still older Green Room, adapted, in 1890 or thereabouts, for keeping the " properties." You will not find the same prompt corner where once Mr. Allen, the prompter, used to have his clock and the minute book into which he recorded faithfully the precise moment when each curtain rose and fell, how many " calls " had been taken, and many things besides. In this corner was a specially hot pipe (water, I suppose), round which Mr. Allen would pile a few well-selected potatoes at about 7:45 each evening — the which he would shift at about 8:40, or after the rise of the curtain on the second act — shifting them again and yet again as each act came round, and thus baking them to a turn. I cannot remember that he ever offered me a potato at the end of an evening, so I suppose he baked these all for himself and Mrs. Allen, and any Miss or Master Allen that existed: I never knew if any of these did exist — to me he was Old Allen, and there could not possibly be any Old Miss Allen or Old Master Allen. Allen prompted — I suppose he prompted; he was always very intent on the book (and the potatoes!) as soon as the curtain rose, but I cannot recall him prompting anyone except Ellen Terry — who never had the same sure grasp of her words that she had on her public.

Allen also held the prompt book at rehearsals — and did a good deal of good hard work — but it is less what he did than the sound of his name which reminds me of him. The sound of Irving calling " Allen " is what I hear even now. Then Allen would trot up and would begin to write something down in the prompt book — "Five spears, not three here, Allen" — down it went into the book — "*Five spears not three*" — "*G*" — standing for "Guvnor."

Mr. Allen also acted now and again — notably as the *Postillion* in *The Lyons Mail*, in which character he has been immortalized by James Pryde in his portrait of Irving as *Dubosc* — a masterly painting which will live on for ever. Old Allen also played the *Lord Mayor* in *Richard III* (1877). So far as I have been able to discover, he did not act in any other production — nor did he repeat his impersonation of the *Lord Mayor of London* when *Richard III* was revived in 1897.

It was in this revival of *Richard III* that I " created," as it is called, my last new part with Irving — that of the sickly *King Edward IV,* in which character I had the supreme satisfaction and puzzlement of seeing my master on his knee before me. To be able to say that once to me " Irving bent the knee " — what a delirious moment — the pinnacle of my career as an actor; and on the very boards of the Lyceum Theatre, too — if it hadn't seemed to me so gloriously funny, I'd have put on a few airs afterwards.

There was no afterwards, for that was the first and last night of the run. (When the run of *Richard III* was resumed the following year, I was not there to play the part of *Edward IV:* I had grown ambitious, and was searching for a way to begin the work I have been doing since.) That same night, after the performance, Irving slipped on his stairway in Grafton Street, and ruptured the ligaments under the knee-cap. People have whispered that he had drunk too well: people who whisper that sort of rubbish of men who know how to carry any amount are generally teetotallers, incapable of carrying one half-glass of barley-water. "Honest Iago" repeats it, by saying that he or

15A Grafton Street, Bond Street, where Irving lived from 1872 to 1899

someone had it from one of Irving's sons. It is so improbable that Harry or Laurence Irving could say any such thing, that we may dub the inventor a liar straight away. Anyhow, Iago in his vanity, is happy to have passed along a lie. Someday you will find this lie in writing, and it will perhaps surprise a few to note the name of the scribe.

I once saw Irving apparently intoxicated — after eating a small steak, and drinking nothing. It was about two in the morning, and it was in the Beef Steak Room — and there he lay back in his chair, saying very little — dog-tired after a nine-hour semi-dress-rehearsal. As we know, food has the same effect on a man who has laboured as he did that evening, as half a wine-glass of Lager beer would have upon Mr. Bernard Shaw. I watched him, and wondered what was the matter: that was all that was the matter — dog-tired. It was the only time in many years' experience of him that I ever saw him so dog-tired.

ANOTHER corner of the Lyceum Theatre which now no longer looks its old self, is the O. P. corner — or opposite prompt. There, night after night, stood a very tall and muscular man, whose name I am sorry to have forgotten, and whose task was to control the guide rope which held in place the immense roller of the curtain, as it slapped its way down its forty-feet drop. Roller curtains are now out of fashion — they were once important for many a reason, the least of these being that they kept one nicely in touch with the eighteenth century. These rollers were hollow, and fixed to the lower end of the big drop curtain used in most theatres during the *entr' actes*. At the beginning of the evening, this curtain was not visible, for in front of it was that famous green baize curtain which, rising, revealed the drop curtain, painted beautifully by Hawes Craven.

The roller on such a curtain would be distinctly heavy; two thick ropes which wound themselves round each end of the roller as it descended, unwound themselves as it was pulled up — counter weights raised it, and a big wheel worked by two men lowered it; I believe this was the action, though I cannot be positive. One of the many large wheels up in the flies above the stage, controlled this immense sheet of painted canvas, with its hollow roller — which roller, when it touched the stage, touched it so lightly, one would have thought that many hands were lowering it gently, as though it were a box containing glass. Modern electrical engineers have simplified all the complications of the stage mechanism, have improved it in eighty ways out of a hundred, but have lost us at least twenty advantages — and I count the roller curtain as one of the minor advantages lost to the stage.

You could time it so well — it came under more perfect control, somehow, than any other curtain ever has done — its descent could be rapid or lingering — its slight thud as it touched the stage lent a certain finality to the scene, as a full stop does to a sentence. The swift descents were thrilling as an experience, if you stood in the O. P. corner — twice as thrilling to the O. P. limelight man on his perch some fifteen to twenty feet above the stage, for the roller slapped its way past him and his lamp, and the lamp sometimes protruded a little; and the job that the O. P. guardian at the guide rope had to do was to steer it safely past man and lamp. Just as it got by, it came rushing down on us beneath — we had to squeeze back a little, and there it was lying on the floor at last — but only to ascend rapidly the next moment, for the "call."

Although it was forbidden to sit on the roller, I have now and again seen a famous person or two resting on it in an interval, and watching the new scene being set. Mr. Gladstone would have a chair whenever he sat in the O. P. corner to watch a performance, and a red curtain would be draped round and above him. He never sat on the curtain in the *entr'actes;* but then he was austere, and also very aged, the time I saw him behind the scenes — held his hand to his ear the whole time to catch every word — and turned it towards each speaker in turn: the acting seemed to interest him less than the words. He looked like an eagle, only his eyes seemed more brilliant. Yes, very like an eagle in crouching position, poise of head on shoulders, and beak. The eyebrows were terrific. Why was he, too, made out to be so very saintly — pictured as calmly divine — when every line of his face revealed a volcanic power which we associate with all that is satanic? Can't *anyone* be allowed to be crowned with laurels in England, unless first made out to be that thing so detestable to Laurence Irving and many of us — " the white-winged angel "? I saw Gladstone there in 1890, during the performance of *Ravenswood,* and again in 1891, when *Much Ado About Nothing* was running; and a third time in 1892, during *Henry VIII.* With Gladstone in the O. P. corner and Mr. Allen in the P. corner, what more could be desired?

Section of Tallis' View of London showing Wellington Street, Strand

THESE two corners were not more thrilling than a third corner of the Lyceum Theatre: for in that corner was a big, open, winding staircase, which led to Irving's dressing-room. I have dozens of visions of Irving descending this staircase — it never changed, but there he was coming down in red as *Mephisto* on one night, on another in brown as *Mathias,* or in black as *Dr. Primrose,* or in pale blue as *Louis XI.* He always dressed in his large private room at the top of these stairs — about fifteen or twenty stairs, split up into three parts, with a bit of a passage to traverse, too — and one would have thought that he would tire of these continual up and down trips night

Henry Irving's dressing room at the Lyceum Theatre. Drawn in
1900 by one of his company.

after night — but he kept to it to the end of his time. He could have annexed space from the stage floor and built himself a new dressing-room, but I take it he rather liked the quietness of the retreat, although to reach it and emerge from it cost him a good deal of extra time and fatigue . . . having to pass up or down about twelve times in the course of an evening — twenty-four in a double performance: seven times a week would bring this up to about eighty-four, and adding rehearsals, we can pretty surely reckon it at a hundred times that he wasted strength on this unnecessary voyage to and from that room.

Tallis' View of London showing Burleigh Street, Strand

It had, I believe, two windows, looking on to Burleigh Street — facing the public house. These two windows were heavily curtained, and his dressing-table was before the left-hand window — but perhaps my sketch of the room, made in 1900, will serve to give as good a notion as any description. Behind the paper-basket is a large mirror, which reflects a small screened-off washing place at that end of the room which we cannot see.

Into this dressing-room everyone would not be allowed: only those people Irving liked, or had immediate need of speaking to. Stoker, of course — Ellen Terry — Loveday — Coquelin — Sarah Bernhardt — Pollock — Pinero —

all artists, and a few dramatic critics: and here it was that his faithful valet, dresser, and wig-maker, all in the one person of Walter — Mr. Walter Collinson — flitted silently, working all the time, unseen and unheard, the only essential person besides the Chief. He was an old friend of mine, and is the next person I think of whenever I think of H. I. I am pretty certain that few men were more heroic in the eyes of their valets than this impersonator of all the double-dyed villains in the dramatic world.

It is curious that Irving should shine best in villain's parts, and it is also curious that villainy itself shone at its best when he interpreted one of its representatives. *Louis XI* was a villain, but assuredly I preferred him to *Charles I* — *Mathias* was a murderer, and yet he delighted me far more than did *Richelieu* — *Mephistopheles* was a joy, while *Edgar Ravenswood* was, after all, rather dreary.

Irving as *Dr. Primrose* in the stage version of *The Vicar of Wakefield,* was all that the ideal vicar of our countryside has been and ever will be — kindly — a little fussy — calm — mild in voice and gentle in movement — the perfection of what we call a good man. Yet I recall how at rehearsal he once made an exit, bleating softly like a sheep, " Baa — baaa — baaaa " — in self-criticism of his way of over-painting a sanctity he could not quite believe in — a doddering sanctity, allied to the perfectly mild — the awfully good. Irving as a man was all that was good, but he wasn't mild — he was, if one can picture such a thing, a good Mephistopheles.

As a host, he performed the part of Irving with much charm.

I suppose that no reader for one moment imagines that my insistence on Irving being nothing but an actor implies in any way some belittlement, and that in the back of my head I have some thought that it may be counted against him in the future. Whoever should chance to think such a thought, let him rid himself of it at once.

This man was of such singleness of purpose, like a beautiful dog with eyes fixed, nose pointing — terrifying to some, because of its concentration. And this concentration was apparent even after working hours, and when comfortably seated entertaining his friends in the Beef Steak Room, once the ancient Beef Steak Club, which was situated somewhere at the back of the Lyceum Theatre.

I was privileged to be at many of these suppers, between the ages of eighteen and twenty-five. Something of my education took place in this room. Nothing amused Irving so much as to poke fun at one or two of us, so as to bring us out. It thrilled rather than hurt any young fellow, because we really all loved him very much, in spite of the fact that we took his hard-earned gold as though we were earning it ourselves, and returned very little — for we possessed not so much of talent, after all.

Besides the lessons of the sharp, kindly tongue, there was the experience of sitting among some of the most interesting and famous people of that time. On rare occasions there would be present great ones of the realm. I remember distinctly one very great one. She came with her mother and her brother, and sat at table with those who were later on to become her subjects . . . I think the date was May 26, 1891.

It was a charming old place, this panelled Beef Steak Room — not too large, but somehow more of a little hall than a room, and yet cosy. Pictures of actors all around, each picture lighted above or beneath with shaded lights; and a large supper table practically filling the whole room.

You reached this delightful haven from the stage, by mounting long staircases, which might belong to some dusty building of the time of Dickens — anything but a primrose way. It was so peculiarly of a theatre, this old magic room, lighted up gaily with candles — unless I've dreamt the candles.

Among other celebrated people who came to the Lyceum as Irving's guests, there were three who were particular friends of my mother, but whom I never met in the Beef Steak Room. These were Alfred Gilbert, Oscar Wilde, and Burne-Jones. All three were her devoted admirers.

Except at the Lyceum I never saw any of these three famous men. It was a time of enchantment, these Lyceum days. The kindliness of Burne-Jones, his timid but thrilled way of coming to the Lyceum to sit in a box and see a play without seeing too much of it; his and my mother's joy at sitting together on the steps of a box when she wasn't on the stage, and talking like children about nothing. And I was allowed to go call a cab for him, and guide him through the twisting passages behind the scenes, with the tricky steps here and bits of slope there. I remember this well: for I remember that in 1890 Mr. Burne-Jones was as big a name as any in that Victorian world, and I was brought up to worship his work.

Wilde and my mother seemed less like children, and more like a pair of fools — proposing impossible flights to a Covent Garden Masked Ball, or where not — and she maybe in her *Fair Rosamund* costume, and having an act of *Becket* still to play.

"Nellie," I remember he said, "let us go now — go to the Fancy Ball close by." And she: "Oscar, let us go — let us go to the moon."

They understood each other well.

As for Gilbert — with such a sympathy as his, so utterly extravagant when he spoke to anyone who was even faintly an artist, so generously extravagant in all his suggestions, when it was a full-grown artist — fancy his delight and his expression of it to a woman — an actress he admired like Ellen Terry.

All these men were artists, and spirits delightful in every way when they spoke to her, and she too speaking with them. There, there sang short but perfect love songs — so gay, so dear these were.

I was all that time essentially the son of Ellen Terry, and indeed, no three letters would I sooner put after my name today, were I allowed to, than "*S. E. T.*" But in those days I felt like a nobody running after a somebody. Who saw her, I saw too, as a rule: who wrote to her I heard of.

IRVING'S WAY

ALL THROUGH this entertainment at the Lyceum by Irving, paced a certain stiffness, for all its hospitality — a certain something which young and over-sensitive beings could not quite say was jolly — and this was because of that strange thing which we can call " Irving's way."

Irving's way was very curious. He certainly inherited some strange demon or other, which put terror into people.

I think I know what it was that did this. It is the oddest thing in the world that it should be what I think it was.

It is customary for actors to act both on the stage and off it. Should you ever think to become an actor, you will try to do both. Even men and women who are not actors, act sometimes in their daily life. They do it so well that they deceive each other. Some do it to gain things: place, power, or wealth: others do it to give things — to give without our seeing. But most actors who act off the stage do it for a very vague reason, and do it so badly that their performance is positively uninteresting. Henry Irving did it because it never entered his head to do anything else. He never allowed any other thought than the stage to enter his head.

If he sat in a garden, the garden became a stage — any point in the garden that might be of any slight value to him later on, he made a mental note of. When making this mental note, he had a peculiarly concentrated, yet far-

away look about him. It was not only in his face — it was
all over him. It was not put on — not acting in that sense
— but it was such a concentrated essence of love for that
to which he had devoted his soul, that it became positively
terrifying, unless by chance you knew what it was he was
thinking of, seeing, hearing, and noting.

It was this strange way of his which people felt to be
mysterious, for people seldom encountered such singleness
of purpose. It is not easy to conceive a person who from
morn until night shall think of one thing only, see one
thing only, and allude to everything in terms of that one
thing.

If someone showed him a picture, Irving saw in it only
that which he could use, maybe scenically or in some other
way on his stage. Play a sonata or sing a song for him,
and he listened and thought solely of how to apply that
to the Lyceum Theatre. When it was over, he would say
something about the music, with this thought of the stage
at the back of his mind; and if you referred what he said
to anything but the stage — and everybody did that —
then it seemed mysterious in the highest degree.

The round, green-painted table at which I am writing
this, is, to everyone who will see it, an ordinary round
green table: but to Irving it would be something in the
third act of *The Merchant of Venice, Othello,* or *Jingle*
— it is quite probable, this. And this was rather terrifying, if you come to think of it: it was as strange and wonderful as that thing which we are told is woman's whole
existence, and it was something like that.

Saying that Irving acted off the stage, I would not have

any young person suppose he carried on like a clown, or was anything at all " theatrical," in the gaudy sense of the word. He acted the plainest Englishman that has ever been known. A plain suit of clothes covered him: no one would ever note what it was he wore — it was so plain: it was at the same time perfect. No one would remark on the curious way he walked, because in the street he walked with perfect street plainness. His feet, which, as I have said already, he caused to execute strange dances during a performance, merely glided along unobtrusively, when walking from Grafton Street down to the Garrick Club. His control over his feet was very marked, if you watched it closely; but then, so was the control over the rest of his person: no person was better controlled. You know how there is something of that about a very fine churchman. What is it? Nothing angular — no jerks — never an error in a single gesture. It is the discipline of the body: that helped to create this strange " way " of Irving.

It was not " strange " as Iago means it, uttering it between gusts of breezy laughter, so ill assumed. He was quite a simple man — he picked up a cup of tea just the same as you or I — he drank it, I assure you, without making a noise — he never threw down the cup — he ate toast without quoting from Shakespeare. It is true that he did not slouch along the street in an everyday way: he walked and talked with distinction — but he made very casual remarks, often of little or no importance, some of which are recorded as though equal in value to the prophetic utterances of Isaiah. His expressed opinions of people were not always worth very much — because he was not often thinking of them — only of their appearance and manner — and to record all his chance sayings about people, his so-called "malicious digs," is to record the most trivial thing about him; these "digs" should be put in their right place — the waste-paper basket. Irving was not witty like Whistler and Wilde. When he was silent, he was forming opinions which, more often than not, he never put into words. These opinions would take expression at some time or other in the work. Is not this the process by which very many artists live and work? For very many artists are only thoroughly articulate in their work. Quite possibly Irving's unexpressed opinion of Eleonora Duse or of Gothic architecture found expression in his performance of *Thomas Becket* or *Corporal Brewster*, and some subtle interpretation of Sarah Bernhardt, maybe, came out only in his by-play during the third act of his *Mephistopheles*.

I am unaware if anybody ever heard what he thought of these two great actresses who came to London, but I have an opinion that if he was present at any of their performances — and I think he was probably present at one performance of each actress — he never saw them. What I mean is this: that the great things that would move us in a theatre passed over him as being nothing whatever. It wasn't that having seen them, he determined that he would be malicious or funny about such lovely things — it was that *he positively never saw them*. Think of the nature of spectator and actor, and of the immense gulf which separates these two. What, after all, is there for a great actor to see when present at some performance by a great actor? Some technical touch here, some technical touch there . . . some trifle will appeal to him more than something of greater importance. The great actor is the last person who needs to be moved in a theatre — he knows all about the personality: personality is not going to excite him, or cause him wonderment. The way another actor may disguise his whole appearance — that, too, is not going to astonish him. He is not going to be deceived in any way by the tricks of a trade which sets out to deceive: and you never saw a clown sitting in front, who laughed at another clown because he made his jokes pat, and fell on his back neatly. What he may do is to count how long it takes for his friend to make the joke — the time he takes, that may interest him. He won't find anything funny in his face, and yet all of us around the circle are screaming with laughter. In fact we are a good audience, and a great actor cannot be a good audience. Maybe it is for this reason that the great Salvini, whose memory I revere, writes so wretchedly about Irving in his *Memoirs*. When I was an actor, I could not appreciate an evening at a theatre as I did when I ceased to act — now that I have not acted for many years, I count myself one of the best spectators living.

The second thing which might easily prevent Irving from being able to pass any but the most casual opinion on a fellow-actor, would be that he never gave a fig for an opinion expressed on his own acting; praise or blame had no effect on him — so what effect would it have, he asked himself, on any other actor, if that actor were a sensible man? He always liked to hope that every actor

was at least a sensible man. If disappointed by some trifle
in any performance, he confined himself to the brief sentence, " Demmed bad actor "; but I think I never heard
him say " A demmed good actor " : and I now and again
accompanied him to a theatre — to see Wilson Barrett in
The Sign of the Cross, and Coquelin in *L'Ami Fritz,* for
example. And when he said an actor was bad, he was
really perturbed and troubled, cross that a man should be
such a damn bad actor — he wasn't critical, he was not
wishing to express an opinion — he was really troubled,
and very quiet. He would look on other actors somewhat
in the same way that St. Francis looked on the Franciscans.
There before them lay their path — clearly indicated —
and dammé, hardly one of them following it. " I found
an Order," says St. Francis, " I provide a roof to cover our
heads; I go away to attend to the sick, and on returning, I
find everybody in feather beds and making themselves
comfortable. What do you want to be comfortable for if
you are a Franciscan? " And so it was with Irving —
" What do you want with approval or disapproval, if you
are an actor? " For it meant the whole of this world and
the next, with Irving, to be an ACTOR, and in his innocence,
his proud innocence, he supposed it meant as much to
every other performer. I would go so far as to say that
so intense was the fire which burned in him, this belief of
his that the ACTOR was all that really mattered, that he
suffered keenly whenever he found actors taking things
easily, and considering too lightly this thing which to him
was really a sacred trust. It seems queer to you — maybe
it even sounds a little foolish; but believe me, you

who never knew him, it was just this concentrated fanatical joy, bound tight under the control of his immense will, which made him the great being he was — the superlatively great actor many of us knew him to be.

His company adored him — even as the Franciscan Brotherhood adored St. Francis — and though he could never raise a great fire from it, it was proud to serve as a background to his blazing genius. Possibly the shades of some of that company might be heard saying today, " Well, Sir Henry, if I could earn a big salary like you, and be the highly-respected manager of the Lyceum Theatre, with a nice comfortable house off Bond Street, and a host of friends, then perhaps I could look on the profession of actor as you do." But as a matter of fact, Irving had suffered more than any of us — had felt despair more often — had never shirked the hopelessness of any future, and had gone on, and gone with the fires burning and the flags waving: and when he came to be so celebrated, so successful, Irving had little more money than when unknown and alone, for the money had gone into the work; and the responsibility of being manager of the Lyceum was one of the most accursed responsibilities anybody could wish to have — not a happiness: it was a fierce joy to this furnace with a will to preserve the old ideal — but not exactly a happiness.

Irving was not a happy man, in the sense that a sanguine disposition finds a man happy and helps to keep him so: he was happy only through an " ecstasy of will." Difficulties alone made him happy. It was through this

" ecstasy of will " (I take the expression from Nietzsche, an enemy of mine from whom I have learnt something), that his performances became inspired. In this sense his inspiration had that about it which seemed forced, and that forced inspiration is the inspiration of the spirit. It is only people who never saw Irving act, who speak of his performance as " gentlemanly," " cultured," " intellectual." And possessing this power of forcing his soul to which Shakespeare refers, he, in sheer relief, enjoyed most the acting of those players who used no force at all. If ever he was happy, it was in contemplating that gayer — maybe lesser — thing.

It was this which made him choose Ellen Terry to be his leading lady. I remember him telling me, at Canterbury, at supper late one night, after I had been fussing about on the stage, doing thoughtful things in a part which needed dash and little else — I remember him saying that geniality was the greatest gift an actor could possess. He meant to say that probably I had inherited a measure of geniality, and that I should be a fool to attempt to think out every gesture of my performance — and I *had* been thinking them out that evening, and he had been present. He didn't say to me, " It is the soul, my boy — force the soul ": he didn't say, in other words, " Do as I have done "; that evening he was on holiday, and certainly he was not thinking of himself.

When he selected Ellen Terry as his leading lady, he was thinking of himself, of course, about as much as Hamlet thought of Laertes when, on crossing swords, he cries gallantly —

*I'll be your foil, Laertes; in mine ignorance Your skill shall,
like a star i' the darkest night, Stick fiery off indeed.*

And it is to be noted that Irving did not change his leading lady (a managerial custom often of an afternoon): it
was his leading lady who, feeling, quite without warrant,
that she was growing old, lest she should impede him left
him to go on alone.

I have always wondered who it was that ever started the
idiotic question (and kept the question fresh, too), " Was
Irving really a great actor? " and why other people tried
to delude the world into believing that he was a great
artist, a great personality, a great anything you like, but
not a great actor. As well say the same of Ellen Terry —
and they *do* say it — that she was not a great actress — that
she was a great woman, a great dear, and that she had a
great heart. To me it seems quite simple that if anybody
can play the fourth act of *Ophelia,* that scene which is
called the " mad scene," as Ellen Terry did, that person is
indubitably a great actress. I have seen I know not how
many people play this scene, and they were ridiculous. I
can recall scenes from *Much Ado About Nothing,*
played by Ellen Terry, and from *The Merchant of
Venice,* both of which I have seen performed in Europe by
people who were considered skilled actresses, but who had
not even begun to know what it means to act. Ellen Terry
was very much a daughter of Shakespeare, and when she
spoke his prose it was as though she but repeated something she had heard at home — something said that morning. It seemed the easiest thing in the world to do, and the
unskilful part of the world supposed that it was as easy as

it seemed, and that, being easy, it could not be acting — it must be what is called "natural." And it was another unskilful section of the same public which, finding Irving forcing the soul, said, "That is so unnatural that it cannot be acting — there is no art in that." The truth is, I suppose, that at certain hours certain people enter the theatre in very uncertain moods, and *rather* liking this, *rather* disliking that, and thoroughly bored with life, they come across something which is markedly what it is, and that is too much for them altogether, and — cheering up at last — they express their positive displeasure emphatically.

Thus it was that the unskilful found Ellen Terry no actress because so natural; Irving no actor, because so unreal — but never were these critics able to explain how it was that the huge audiences were so hushed to listen — so still, watching — nor why, when the curtain fell, there came from this undemonstrative old British public a roar of uncontrollable enthusiasm, a torrent of applause, a waving of handkerchiefs and hats, and the cries of " Bravo ! Bravo ! ! "

BUT I have wandered from the street, and brought you into the theatre again.

I feel conscious that I am not doing this immense subject anything like full justice — nor am I able to do better. And yet I will not apologize for my shortcomings as a writer, since writing is not my craft. What I have ever written has been put down swiftly — then worked over and over: sometimes it went easily, sometimes it creaked. Here, as it creaks, I groan — I feel as Marc Antony felt when defending Cæsar from the over-righteous rascals of that day.

But if I splutter and cannot find the right word, put it down to something that's good, anyhow; . . . listen how glibly one of his foes will coin phrases to his harm, . . . will lie like truth.

Now to return to the subject.

IRVING used very few words in daily speech: would repeat a few essential words — repeat them in measured tones. He repeated because he wished there to be no doubt in the mind of the listener — if the listener had any mind — what it was that he was saying so very briefly.

There are many stories which we have heard about Irving which illustrate this, and when they are told by some actor, or by someone with the actor's talent, they become intensely interesting; but when written, they are of less account.

Speaking with people in private life — with one, two or more, he always quite simply held them to be spectators in the theatre. The voice would do surprising things in order to hold the attention of these people. The attention was never to wander, and having secured it, he rapidly made his point in such an incisive tone that it left everyone who heard it for the first time, not a little startled.

That there was something of Edmund Kean in Irving is testified to by Sir William Fraser, in his book, *Disraeli and his Day;* and it is testified to in a curious roundabout way — at the beginning of his book, and later on at the end. The book, published in 1891, consists of fragment after fragment, bundled in without any particular order: fifteen lines, then a break; twenty lines, then a break, and then eight or ten lines — so on right through. On page fifty-two he comes to Kean and Disraeli — and this is the passage:

I have supposed that Disraeli bore some resemblance, as a young man, to the great actor Edmund Kean; and I have a belief that his style of utterance was not unlike his; in fact, may have been founded upon it.

Following this are 260 pages of similar fragments — and suddenly and for no particular reason, comes this entry on pages 313–14:

The only person whom I have met who reminds me in any way of the manner of Disraeli in private life, is Mr. Henry Irving. When I first had the honour of knowing him, I could not persuade myself that he was not imitating Disraeli's manner: the peculiar slowness and deliberation of utterance; a voice very much of the same timbre; and the resemblance in other minute particulars surprised me. Mr. Irving told me that he had, to his regret, never heard Disraeli speak in Parliament: and, I think, added that he had no personal acquaintance with him.

It is peculiarly interesting that Fraser should imagine the style of Disraeli's utterance was founded upon that of Edmund Kean, and that the slowness and deliberation of Irving's utterance was imitated from Disraeli. Of course it was no such thing — but for all that, it is valuable to us to find Fraser unconsciously connecting the two greatest of English actors — the one who died in 1833, the other born five years later.

IRVING'S END, AND AFTER

AND NOW it is twenty-six years since the death of Henry Irving, if you count from the day when the public heard he was dead, at Bradford; but if you count from the real day he died, it is longer — it is thirty-two years.

For it was in 1898, to be precise, that he got the first really important stab in the back, and it was in 1902–1903 that he was finished off. In 1898 the Lyceum Theatre, over which he had ruled, and ruled perfectly (no complaints were ever made, so far as I know) — in 1898 the Lyceum capitulated. He had held up the Shakespearean tradition there, the great English tradition — in fact the best tradition of the whole world, best not because it is England's, but because it is and let us hope always will be, the eternal tradition — that of doing work in the best possible way and for the best possible ideals. In that year of disgrace, in 1898, the Lyceum Theatre made a fool of itself; and it was London's business men who rendered it foolish. They turned it into the Lyceum Limited Liability Company; and they could so easily have turned it into the National Theatre. So obvious and so easy, one would have thought, considering how many men of power and wealth had for twenty-seven years been Irving's guests at this same Lyceum. A glance at Brereton's *Life of Irving* shows the numbers of friends he had, and how much support he could — one supposes

— have counted on. Roughly speaking, it was the whole of the influential part of Great Britain.

But he and his friends were thinking at cross purposes. He was artist, but he was also manager, and he had so incessantly insisted upon one thing — that theatre work is to be judged by the receipts. Naturally an artist does not want to talk about his art, or ever to go with another along that path, to tread which is to disturb the soul, going with any but his own secret thoughts: and thus it is that very often an artist will start strange phantom hares; and the hare that Irving started — this Mad March Hare, "annual receipts" — had grown to such gigantic proportions by the year 1898, that everyone followed after it. And so (presumably) they thought that he *preferred* that the Lyceum should be turned into a Limited Liability Company, since he could not very rapidly find men prepared, on their own initiative, and in spite of this nighthare, to establish the place as the National Theatre, and invite Irving to resume his former position as head and front of the whole affair.

It really is a little more than astonishing that the people allowed him to fool around with a Limited Liability Company, because anybody in his senses must have known that it was destined to fail. Limited Liability Companies are all right for shops; but for an affair like Irving and the Lyceum Theatre, they simply will not work — and this one did not work.

No artist of his magnitude could brook interference in any way. He was of the same type as Napoleon in sensitiveness — I claim no other resemblance for him — and you will remember that the moment anybody questioned Napoleon he fell to pieces, stuttered and spluttered and lost his head. Especially that day on which he appeared before the Five Hundred — that ridiculous Liability Company of France. Having soldiers, Buonaparte made a sign, and the Five Hundred were put out of action: but an artist has no soldiers — he may not assault those who oppose him — and I have never known why, if one man may do it, another man may not. If force as the final argument is permissible in politics, why the deuce is it not permissible in theatres? I should very much like to bombard a couple of theatres in London and raze them to the ground, because I should be doing the nation a great service; but if I did so, I should be arrested — whereas if any statesman should wish to use force to carry out some doubtful political reform, and if his men could shoot straight, he would be hailed as the saviour of the country. It is a little odd, is it not? And it is queer that artists, who are pretty well all the time something like the saviours of their epoch, or the epoch after them, may not do more. Since Irving was doing no harm, was trying to pour out good all the time, and doubtless exerting a spiritual influence over the nation which was of considerable value — it is strange that when he wished to continue to do this, he should have been impeded: heckled by a pack of shareholders, who call out from the back of a room: " What about the threepence spent on the programmes? How about that six bob tip to the porter? "

It is when such petty things can happen in Europe in connection with great endeavour that all the accumulated

Entrance to the New Queen's Theatre — Long Acre. From a photograph taken in 1927. The letters A RE on the door are the only sign remaining that it was a theatre.

By courtesy of the publishers of "The Mask."

experience of our forefathers seems wasted, this being permitted.   And not only permitted, but encouraged: for artists are even solemnly urged to enter into an alliance with such fatuous shareholders, and told that three penny notions are worth more than one golden one.   Golden notions all along the line are said to belong to the past, to be fantastic: and no nation can possibly find a guinea — three-pence, oh yes.   This might happen anywhere, in any epoch — but it happens over and over again in ours. The gentlemen in England when Irving should have been placed at the head of a National Theatre — that was in 1898 — evidently had not even sufficient pride to wish to see any National Theatre.   This must be the truth.

But suppose it not true — allow that there is and always will be enough pride in England — allowing this, then it merely means that they were listening to Mr. William Archer, Mr. Shaw, Brutus, Cassius, and all of 'em, who were running Irving down day by day, behind his back.

So the National Theatre never came into existence, and Irving went out of existence because of that.

At the death of Irving, everybody at once overestimated his importance and underestimated his value, and this is still underestimated.   Those who did the first, strove to keep alive a so-called " Irving tradition," which in actuality had not had time to become a tradition.   They propped up their theatres by doing as he had been doing, and used the same props.   There were a few of them who did this excellently well, and these found that it was profitable to do that — and profit is a mighty potent argument. Was not this same profit the very essence of the supposed

Irving teaching? Though here it is as well to realize that what these imitators took from Irving was, after all, only what he had taken from Charles Kean. The lavish style of staging — the historical accuracy — the handling of crowds — in short, the flashy part of Kean's "scholarly" stage-management. What they did not and could not take from Irving, was the one thing that made this kind of production alive — his coming into it.

Since, then, there existed no Irving round whom this kind of production could be built, it really was but a small, catch-penny thing to do, to follow the method. From a business point of view it was not the wrong thing to do, and sure enough, before long people began to speak of these able followers of Irving (followers in the sense of those who follow the *pattern,* since they are not keen to follow the spirit) in terms of the very highest respect. They are nearly all dead and gone, and so, after all, one can but congratulate them on the good luck they met with, but which at the time one hoped would be denied to them. Such was the power of Irving and the Kean-Irving method of theatre running, it even carried the followers along to success after both men were dead. Yes, they were exceedingly successful; succeeding while the Theatre itself suffered, and I am afraid there is no denying this. A new public was coming along which had rarely gone to see Irving, and it was now told that it could see the same sort of thing at five or six theatres — you know the catchword: "Jones's Grates are just as good" — and so the new public was deceived, and the usual thing happened: the old die-hard Irvingites retired to their homes,

and avoided the theatres — the followers
disbanded — some took new masters, and otn.
strike out for themselves. New masters or n.
mained loyal to their old leader — let no mistake be
on this point.

But the affection for Irving, and the admiration for his
achievement, and the grief at his death were all so sincere, that some of the public, critics, and actors, were led
to commit the error of believing that no good could possibly come along now that Irving was no more. This was
hero-worship turned foolish, but it was affection and admiration which led them to it. Even these extremists do
not merely grieve that our beloved Chief is not here with
us: were it that only, one could indeed sympathize: but
they express a stolid despair, a pessimistic conviction that
it is quite impossible for anything good to happen to the
British stage, since Irving is not here to make it happen —
which is, to put it quite plainly, rubbish.

As a matter of fact, even as Irving was passing, a new
movement was on foot. The detractors of this movement,
headed by Bernard Shaw again, began misrepresenting
us at once. Mr. Shaw has always been a sincere enemy to
the Theatre, and one who innocently bears false witness
against most artists, so it is only fair to state here that we
thoroughly misled him, and he fell into the trap.

In some of our manifestos, we frightened a few playwriters into supposing that we wanted to prevent them
from earning a fair wage in the Theatre. We announced
that we could do without plays — what was the spoken
word, we asked — and why write the spoken word —

why not invent it and speak it, and do without scribblers? All of which did no harm to the pocket of any playwriter, and it is useless for playwriters to pose as martyrs, when only recently it was announced that in three years one London theatre alone had paid £134,000 in authors' fees for three plays only. "*These fees are £45,000 more than was paid on the production and renewals of the same three plays in those three years.*" It therefore will not do for critics to cry out that the producer is a danger to the stage, and the playwriter is an innocent little darling. For to profit at the Theatre's expense — to impoverish the stage by demanding such immense fees as the playwriter gets, is to be a real danger — whereas no amount of scenical fall-lalls can be a real danger: they only add a bit more fun or fancy to any show — and shows do need brightening up a bit. Besides, the new movement was not all scenic — I will tell you what it was.

It was the eternal old and good movement coming once more to life: it was the attempt to revitalize our European Theatre from within — to put it in a sentence, it was to wake up ourselves, and to wake up our house. It was doing in our way what Irving had done in his.

If that be a bad thing to do, then we have done something we shall come to regret — but that it was a good thing to do, seems to have been proved conclusively, by the gradual, increasing acceptance of our work in Europe and America, and the appreciation accorded our productions — and even some of our far-fetched theories.

Before I go on, I must very reluctantly confess that

in England our movement has not yet flourished, and this is perhaps my fault. I was the only one in 1900 who was breaking free in England, so I represent this movement in our land, and I am so constituted that since 1904 I have very wantonly spent far too much time throwing challenges to the old Theatre, instead of getting hold of one playhouse and steadily establishing proof upon proof of the excellence of our ideas and plans. Besides this, I have been far too eager to study the European Theatre, and have travelled to Russia, to Germany, France, Holland, Scandinavia, and Italy, doing this. I have taken to those foreign countries ideas which have contributed a good deal towards improving their work since 1904. It was an Englishman who took them these ideas, so do not forget it. But do not, also, forget that I took them there because I was not able to find any place in England wherein to deposit them safely, to try them out, and to develop them for England.

But lest, from what I say, it be wrongly supposed that any Englishman can lay claim to having inspired the entire European Theatre, let us remember that in all the lands I visited I found remarkable men or women, with brilliant ideas of their own, which they were putting into practice in either a small or a big theatre — a hired playhouse, or one built by or for them: or wandering round as I was doing, spreading their ideas and getting little or much in return for them. Two I place apart — Isadora Duncan and Appia. After these, Stanislavsky, Reinhardt, Mayerhold, Fortuny, Roller, Linnebach, Diagileff and his troupe were early at work, and since these

came the followers — Copeau, Pitoeff, Tairoff, Kommisar-
jevsky, Piscator, Jouvet, Baty and others.[1] One of these
might be an actor, another a designer, a third a producer,
a fourth an impresario; rarely a creator, a real child of
the Muses — I have known only two such, and of these
I shall write some day — but all, great and small, were
eager to express things dramatic in a new way. Irving
had expressed in a new way — in his way — and I, his
pupil, followed his lead. A new way of looking at an old
thing — this was our principal idea, and this idea has
already freshened up that tawdry part of entertainment
which was growing dull — the scenic part — and is slowly
influencing the acting, dancing, singing, and even play-
making. In America, ever since Da Ponte landed there
at the close of the eighteenth century, there have been
pioneers eager to discover for New York a new art or two.
So that quick to follow the banner raised in Europe in
1900 and earlier, have been young American architects,
painters, and even theatre men.

Ours was no hideous revolution — no pompous reform:
we just made some ordinary and desirable changes, and
we have not finished yet.[2]

And it is this new movement — the English section

[1] I mention no playwriters, for the new movement included none —
we were convinced that all playwriters wrote to perfection.

[2] Maybe you will want to know something of this new movement, which
advances, yet never leaves its hold of the ancient traditions. If so, get one or
all of these three books: *The Development of the Theatre,* by Allardyce Nicoll,
M.A. (Harrap); *The Story of the Theatre,* by Glenn Hughes (Samuel
French, Ltd.); and *The Theatre — Three Thousand Years,* by Sheldon
Cheney (Longmans). Nicoll and Hughes both give selected bibliographies
of books which will tell you more: I think it will surprise you to note how
vast is the literature on this subject. None of these books is dull reading, and
all are illustrated — Nicoll giving 271 illustrations, and Cheney 204.

of it — that gives its salute to Irving as having inspired it, and will remain at the salute; and in these pages that I have written, and am now closing, I have wanted to express this — somehow to let it be felt that we are still continuing the tradition, not of Irving alone, but of the other giants who preceded him, and whom he revered. Our new movement is destined to win through. It requires just exactly what Irving required, the lack of which killed him, because he could not get it. Briefly, it requires good support. But our movement is young, and if it does not get that support, it is still going to win: and among the things which are going to help it to win, are its affection and respect for Henry Irving. Henry Irving was the full stop to a period in a long chapter of the stage's history — we have begun a new chapter.

EPILOGUE

SCENES FROM " THE BELLS," " LOUIS XI," AND
" THE LYONS MAIL "

IRVING was essentially an actor, not an orator. While every sentence of a rôle was to him of the utmost importance, he was ever mindful to act before he spoke, and then to follow up the words by acting again.

Before a phrase or a word, Irving would always do something, so that the spectator should never be in doubt as to what the phrase or word was intended to mean; and he gave words special meanings. He was an actor, and not the playwriter's puppet.

In plays where the meaning was only too clear — the words too blunt and dull — Irving acted before and after these words so as to give them an Irving significance. Sometimes a whole scene was merely a succession of things done — acting, with the poor words used as props which hold up plants. Then it was we all drew up to attention — then we were moved — then we understood what it was to be an actor. (Why can't we be helped by some actor to understand this today?)

For example, the last two scenes of *The Bells;* the last scene in *Louis XI;* the last scene in *The Lyons Mail,* though they be well constructed, are not written as Max Beerbohm alone of modern dramatists could have written them. Read these last scenes over to yourself, and you will possibly agree with me. You may even wonder what on earth can be made out of them. Actors know, but you may not know.

It is curious to note that Irving was not bumptious about his acting — one notes it specially here. When the playwright has done his work so astonishingly well that all is plain sailing for the actor (as in that perfect playlet, *A Social Success*), a great actor does not put out his full powers — he is not required to — he does that only when the play is about to collapse. The last scenes of those three plays I have named do not play themselves and, in most hands, they would crumble, and everyone would be rising to go out and get his hat and coat to catch a train home; but for Irving, everyone sat still and could only with the greatest difficulty be persuaded to leave the theatre after the final fall of the curtain — over and over again it had to be raised, for over and over again surged up the feeling of astonishment at his prodigious powers. It was no trick — people were out of themselves, and no longer bothered about trains or trams or the petty loss of an hour. "This is exceptional," said the glow of their faces, the sparkle in their eyes — and they stayed there, a solid theatre-full, and applauded him as they do no actor today.

READ these acts now — if you agree that *The Bells* is not so badly written, you cannot deny that *The Lyons Mail* is awful.

After you have read them, I will add one word more — but that will be directly reported from Irving.

Henry Irving by Bastien LePage. Presented by Miss Ellen Terry to the National Portrait Gallery. *Courtesy of the National Portrait Gallery, London.*

THE BELLS

ACT III [1]

SCENE: *Bedroom in the Burgomaster's House. The whole back of Scene painted on a gauze; alcove on left; door, R.; two windows at back; small table by bed; chair, L.; Night.*

Music: Enter at door, R.; MATHIAS, FATHER WALTER, HANS, CHRISTIAN, ANNETTE, *and* CATHERINE; SOZEL *carrying a lighted candle, bottle of water, and glass, which she places on table; they enter suddenly, the men appear to be slightly excited by wine; lights down at rising of curtain; lights turned up upon entrance of* SOZEL.

HANS (*laughing*). Ha, ha! Everything has gone off admirably. We only wanted something to wind up with, and I may say that we are all as capitally wound up as the great clock at Strasbourg.

WALTER. Yes, and what wine we have consumed! For many a day we shall remember the signing of Annette's marriage contract. I should like to witness such a contract every second day.

HANS. There, I object to your argument. Every day, I say!

CHRISTIAN (*to* MATHIAS). And so you are determined, Mathias, to sleep here tonight.

MATHIAS. Yes, I am decided. I wish for air. I know what is necessary for my condition. The heat was the cause of my accident. This room is cooler, and will prevent its recurrence. (*Laughter heard outside.*)

HANS. Listen, how they are still revelling! Come, Father Walter, let us rejoin the revels!

WALTER. But Mathias already deserts us, just at the moment when we were beginning to thoroughly enjoy ourselves.

---

[1] This is the last act of *The Bells*. The phrases or words in square brackets were changed by Irving. Those in parentheses and underlined are phrases and words substituted by him. There were more, but these are the only ones I can vouch for.

MATHIAS. What more do you wish me to do? From noon till midnight is surely enough!

WALTER. Enough, it may be, but not too much; never too much of such wine.

HANS. There, again, I object to your argument—never enough, I say.

CATHERINE. Mathias is right. You remember that Doctor Zimmer told him to be careful of the wine he took, or it would one day play him false. He has already taken too much since this morning.

MATHIAS. One glass of water before I go to rest is all I require. It will calm me—it will calm me.

(KARL, FRITZ and TONY, *three of the guests of the previous Act, enter suddenly, slightly merry, pushing each other.*)

GUESTS. Good night, Burgomaster. Good night.

TONY. I say, Hans! don't you know that the Night Watchman is below?

HANS. The Night Watchman! What in the name of all that is political, does he want?

KARL. He requires us all to leave, and the house to be closed. It is past hours.

MATHIAS. Give him a bumper of wine, and then good night all!

WALTER. Past hours! For a Burgomaster no regulations ought to exist.

HANS. }
OTHERS. } Certainly not.

MATHIAS (*with fierceness*). Regulations made for all must be obeyed by all.

WALTER (*timidly*). Well, then, shall we go?

MATHIAS. Yes, yes, go! Leave me to myself.

CATHERINE (*to* WALTER). Don't thwart his wish. Follow his directions.

WALTER (*shaking hands with* MATHIAS). Good night, Mathias. I wish you calm repose, and no unpleasant dreams.

MATHIAS (*fiercely*). I never dream. (*Mildly.*) Good night, all. Go, friends, go.

(*Music — Exeunt* WALTER, HANS, *and the three* GUESTS, *saying, " Good night, Burgomaster " —* CATHERINE, AN-NETTE *and* CHRISTIAN *remain.*)

MATHIAS. Good night, Catherine. (*Embracing her.*) I shall be better here. The wine, the riot, those songs have quite dazed my brain. I shall sleep better here, I shall sleep better.
CHRISTIAN. Yes, this room is fresh and cool. Good night.
MATHIAS. The same to you, Christian; the same to you.

(*They shake hands.*)

ANNETTE (*running to her father and kissing him*). Good night, dear father; may you sleep well!
MATHIAS (*kissing her with affection*). Good night, dear child; do not fear for me — do not fear.

(*Music — Exeunt all but* MATHIAS — *Music ceases — he goes up cautiously, locks the door,* R., *and puts the key in his pocket.*)

At last I am alone! Everything goes well. Christian the gendarme is caught! Tonight I shall sleep without a fear haunting me! If any new danger should threaten the father-in-law of the Quarter-master, it would soon be averted. Ah! What a power it is to know how to guide your destiny in life. You must hold good cards in your hands. Good cards! as I have done, and if you play them well you may defy ill fortune.
CHORUS OF REVELLERS *outside,* (*without accompaniment*).
    Now, since we must part, let's drain a last glass;
      Let's drink!
    Let us first drink to this gentle young lass;
      Let's drink!
    From drinking this toast, we'll none of us shrink;
    Others shall follow, when we've time to think.
      Our burden shall be, let us drink!
      The burden to bear is good drink.
                (*Loud laughter heard outside.*)

MATHIAS (*taking off his coat*). Ha, ha, ha! Those jolly topers have got all they want. What holes in the snow they will make before they reach their homes! Drink! Drink! [*Is it not strange? To drink and drown every remorse!*] (How strange to drink and drive away remorse!) Yes, everything goes well! (*He drinks a glass of water.*) Mathias, you can at least boast of having well managed your affairs—the contract signed—rich—prosperous—respected—happy! (*Takes off waistcoat.*) No one now will hear you, if you dream. No one! No more folly!—no more Bells! Tonight, I triumph; for conscience is at rest!

(*He enters the alcove—the* CHORUS OF REVELLERS *heard again, in the distance—a hand is extended from the alcove and extinguishes the candle—stage dark—curtain at back of gauze rises, disclosing an extensive set of a Court of Justice, arched, brilliantly lighted—at back, three* JUDGES *on the bench, dressed in black caps and red robes—at R. and L., the* PUBLIC, *in Alsatian costumes—in front of the* JUDGES, *but beneath them, a table, on which lies the Jew's cloak and cap—on R., the* PUBLIC PROSECUTOR *and* BARRISTERS—*on L., the* CLERK *or* REGISTRAR *of the* COURT, *and* BARRISTERS—*a* GENDARME *at each corner of the Court—* MATHIAS *is discovered seated on a stool in C. of Court—he is dressed in the brown blouse and hood worn by the* MAN *in the vision in Act I—he has his back to the* AUDIENCE, *face to* JUDGES.)

THE CLERK OF THE COURT (*L., standing, reading the Act of Accusation*). Therefore, the prisoner, MATHIAS, is accused of having, on the night of the 24th December 1818, between midnight and one o'clock, assassinated the Jew Kovesky, upon the bridge of Vechem, to rob him of his gold.

PRESIDENT. Prisoner, you have heard the Act of Accusation read; you have already heard the depositions of the witnesses. What have you to say in answer?

MATHIAS (*violently—throws back hood, and starting up*). Witnesses! People who saw nothing; people who live miles from the place where the crime was committed; at night, and in the winter time! You call such people witnesses!

PRESIDENT. Answer with calmness; these gestures—this violence will avail you nothing. You are a man full of cunning.

MATHIAS (*with humility*). No, I am a man of simplicity.

PRESIDENT. You knew well the time to select; you knew well how to evade all suspicion; you knew well how to destroy all direct evidence. You are a dangerous man!

MATHIAS (*derisively*). Because nothing can be proved against me I am dangerous! Every honest man is then dangerous when nothing can be proved against him! A rare encouragement for honesty!

PRESIDENT. The public voice accuses you. Answer me this. How is it that you hear the [*noise*] (sound) of Bells?

MATHIAS (*passionately*). I do not hear the [*noise*] (sound) of Bells! (*Music — Bells heard off as before —* MATHIAS *trembles.*)

PRESIDENT. Prisoner, you speak falsely. At this moment you hear that [*noise*] (sound.) Tell us why is this?

MATHIAS. It is nothing. [*It is simply a jangling in my ears.*] ('Tis but a jangling in mine ears.)

PRESIDENT. Unless you acknowledge the true cause of this noise you hear, we shall summon the Mesmerist to explain the matter to us.

MATHIAS (*with defiance*). It is true then that I hear this [*noise*] (sound.) (*Bells cease.*)

PRESIDENT (*to the* CLERK OF THE COURT). It is well; write that down.

MATHIAS. Yes, but I hear it in a dream.

PRESIDENT. Write, that he hears it in a dream.

MATHIAS (*furiously*). Is it a crime to dream?

THE CROWD (*murmur very softly among themselves, and move simultaneously, each person performing exactly the same movement of negation*). N-N-N-o!

MATHIAS (*with confidence*). Listen, friends! Don't fear for me! All this is but a dream — I am in a dream. If it were not a dream should I be clothed in these rags? Should I have before me such judges as these? Judges who, simply acting upon their own empty ideas, would hang a fellow creature. Ha, ha, ha! It is a dream — a dream! (*He bursts into a loud derisive laugh.*)

PRESIDENT. Silence, prisoner — silence! (*Turning to his companion judges.*) Gentlemen — this [*noise*] (sound) of Bells arises in the prisoner's mind from the remembrance of what is past. The prisoner hears this [*noise*] (sound) because there rankles in his heart the memory of what he would conceal from us. The Jew's horse carried Bells.

MATHIAS. It is false, I have no memories.

PRESIDENT. Be silent!

MATHIAS (*with rage*). A man cannot be condemned upon such suppositions. You must have proofs. I do not hear the [*noise*] (sound) of Bells.

PRESIDENT. You see, gentlemen, the prisoner contradicts himself. He has already made the avowal — now he retracts it.

MATHIAS. No! I hear nothing. (*The Bells heard.*) It is the blood rushing to my brain — [*this*] ('tis but a) jangling in [*my*] (mine) ears. (*The Bells increase in sound.*) I ask for Christian. Why is not Christian here?

PRESIDENT. Prisoner! do you persist in your denial?

MATHIAS (*with force*). Yes. There is nothing proved against me. It is a gross injustice to keep an honest man in prison. I suffer in the cause of justice. (*The Bells cease.*)

PRESIDENT. You persist. Well! Considering that since the affair took place fifteen years have passed, and that it is impossible to throw light upon the circumstances by ordinary means — first, through the cunning and audacity of the prisoner, and second, through the deaths of witnesses who could have given evidence — for these reasons we decree that the Court hear the Mesmerist. Officer, summon the Mesmerist.

MATHIAS (*in a terrible voice*). I oppose it! I oppose it! Dreams prove nothing.

PRESIDENT. Summon the Mesmerist!

(*Exit* GENDARME, *R.*)

MATHIAS (*striking the table*). It is abominable! It is in defiance of all justice!

PRESIDENT. If you are innocent, why should you fear the Mesmerist, because he can read the inmost secrets of your heart? Be calm, or, believe me, your own indiscretion will prove that you are guilty.

MATHIAS. I demand an advocate. I wish to instruct the advocate Linder of Saverne. In a case like this, I do not care for cost. I am calm — as calm as any man who has no reproach against himself. I fear nothing; but dreams are dreams. (*Loudly.*) [*Why is Christian not here?*] (Why is not Christian here?) My honour is his honour! Let him be sent for. He is an honest man. (*With exultation.*) Christian, I have made you rich. Come, and defend me!

(*Music — the* GENDARME *who had gone out, returns with the* MESMERIST.)

MESMERIST (*bending to the Court respectfully*). Your honours, the President and Judges of the Court, it is your decree that has brought me before your tribunal; without such direction, terror alone would have kept me far from here.

MATHIAS. Who can believe in the follies of the Mesmerist? They deceive the public for the purpose of gaining money! They merely perform the tricks of conjurors! I have seen this fellow already at my cousin Bôth's, at Ribeauville.

PRESIDENT (*to the* MESMERIST). Can you send this man to sleep?

MESMERIST (*looking full at* MATHIAS, *who sinks upon chair, unable to endure the* MESMERIST's *gaze*). I can!

MATHIAS (*starting up*). I will not be made the subject of this conjuror's experiments.

PRESIDENT. I command it!

MATHIAS. Christian — where is Christian? He will prove that I am an honest man.

PRESIDENT. Your resistance betrays you.

MATHIAS (*with defiance*). I have no fear. (*Sits.*)

(*The* MESMERIST *goes up-stage to back of* MATHIAS, *makes some passes — Music.*)

MATHIAS (*to himself*). [*Mathias, if you sleep you are lost.*] (Courage, Mathias, if you sleep you're lost.) (*His eyes are fixed as if struck with horror — in a hollow voice.*) No — no — I will not sleep — I — will — (*In a hesitating voice.*) I will — not — no —— (*Falls asleep — Music ceases.*)

MESMERIST (*to the* PRESIDENT). He sleeps. What shall I ask him?

PRESIDENT. Ask him, what he did on the night of the 24th of December, fifteen years ago.

MESMERIST (*to* MATHIAS, *in a firm voice*). You are at the night of the 24th December 1818?

MATHIAS (*in a low voice*). Yes.

MESMERIST. What time is it?

MATHIAS. Half-past eleven.

MESMERIST. Speak on, I command you!

MATHIAS (*still in the same attitude, speaking as if he were describing a vision presented to his sight*). The people are leaving the inn — Catherine and Little Annette have gone to rest. Our man Kasper comes in. He tells me the lime kiln is lighted. I answer him, it is well; go to bed, I will see to the kiln. He leaves me; I am alone with the Jew, who warms himself at the stove. Outside, everything sleeps. Nothing is heard, except from time to time the Jew's horse under the shed, when he shakes his bells.

MESMERIST. Of what are you thinking?

MATHIAS. I am thinking that I must have money — that if I have not three thousand francs by the 31st, the inn will be taken from me. I am thinking that no one is stirring; that it is night; that there are two feet of snow upon the ground, and that the Jew will follow the high road quite alone!

MESMERIST. Have you already decided to attack him?

MATHIAS (*after a short silence*). That man is strong. He has broad shoulders. I am thinking that he would defend himself well, should anyone attack him. (*He makes a movement.*)

MESMERIST. What ails you?

MATHIAS (*in a low voice*). He looks at me. He has grey eyes. (*As if speaking to himself.*) [*I must strike the blow!*] (I'll do it.)

MESMERIST. You are decided?

MATHIAS. Yes — yes; I will [*strike the blow*] (do it!) I will risk it!

MESMERIST. Go on!

MATHIAS (*continuing*). I must, however, look round. I go out; all is dark! It still snows; no one will trace my footsteps in the snow. (*He raises his hand as if feeling for something.*)

MESMERIST. What are you doing?

MATHIAS. I am feeling in the sledge — should he carry pistols! There is nothing — I will [*strike the blow*] (do it!) (*He listens.*) All is silent in the village! Little Annette is crying; a goat bleats in the stable; the Jew is walking in his room!

MESMERIST. You re-enter?

MATHIAS. Yes. The Jew has placed six francs upon the table; I return him his money; he fixes his eyes steadily upon me!

MESMERIST. He speaks to you?

MATHIAS. He asks me how far it is to Mutzig? Four leagues. I wish him well on his journey! He answers — " God bless you!" He goes out — He is gone! (MATHIAS *with body bent, takes several steps forward as if following and watching his victim, he extends his hands.*) The axe! Where is the axe? Ah, here, behind the door! How cold it is. (*He trembles.*) The snow falls — not a star! Courage, Mathias, you shall possess the girdle — courage!

MESMERIST. You follow him?

MATHIAS. Yes, yes. I have crossed the fields! (*Pointing.*) Here is the old bridge, and there below, the frozen rivulet! How the dogs howl at Daniel's farm — how they howl! And old Finck's forge, how brightly it glows upon the hillock. (*Low, as if speaking to himself.*) Kill a man! — kill a man! You will not do that, Mathias — you will not do that! Heaven forbids it. (*Proceeding to talk with meas-*

ured steps and bent body.) You are a fool! Listen, you will be rich, your wife and child will no longer want for anything! [*The Jew came; so much the worse — so much the worse. He ought not to have come!*] You will pay all you owe; you will no more be in debt. (*Loud, in a broken tone.*) It must be, [*Mathias,*] that you kill him! (*He listens.*) No one on the road — no one! (*With an expression of terror.*) What dreadful silence! (*He wipes his forehead with his hand.*) One o'clock strikes, and the moon shines. Ah! (One! One! !) The Jew has [*already*] passed! Thank God! thank God! (*He kneels — a pause — he listens — the Bells heard without as before.*) No! The Bells! The Bells! He comes! (*He bends down in a watching attitude, and remains still — a pause — in a low voice.*) You will be rich — you will be rich — [you will be] rich! (rich!) (*The noise of the Bells increases — the* CROWD *expresses alarm simultaneously — all at once* MATHIAS *springs forward, and with a species of savage roar, strikes a terrible blow with his right hand.*) Ah! ah! I have you now, Jew! (*He strikes again — the* CROWD *simultaneously expresses horror —* MATHIAS *leans forward and gazes anxiously on the ground — he extends his hand as if to touch something, but draws it back in horror.*) He does not move! (*He raises himself, utters a deep sigh of relief, and looks round.*) The horse has fled with the sledge! (*The Bells cease — kneeling down.*) Quick, quick! The girdle! I have it. Ha! (*He performs the action in saying this of taking it from the Jew's body and buckling it round his own.*) [*It is full of gold, quite full.*] (It is full of gold, gold, full of gold, quite full.) Be quick, Mathias, be quick! Carry him away. (*He bends low down and appears to lift the body upon his back; then he walks across stage, his body bent, his step slow as a man who carries a heavy load.*)

MESMERIST. Where are you going?

MATHIAS (*stopping*). To the lime kiln. I am there. (*He appears to throw the body upon the kiln.*) How heavy he was! (*He breathes with force, then he again bends down to to take up a pole — in a hoarse voice.*) Go into the fire, Jew, go into the fire! (*He appears to push the body with the pole, using his whole force, suddenly he utters a cry of horror and staggers away, his face covered with his hands.*) [*Those eyes, oh, those eyes! How he glares at me.*] (Look, look, look, look — those eyes, oh, those eyes! How he glares at me.) (*He sinks on to stool, and takes the same attitude as when first thrown into sleep.*)

PRESIDENT (*with a sign to the* MESMERIST). It is well. (*To the* CLERK OF THE COURT.) You have written all?

CLERK. All!

PRESIDENT (*to* MESMERIST). It is well — awake him now, and let him read himself.

MESMERIST. [*Awake! I command you!*] (*Makes a pass.*)

MATHIAS (*awakes gradually — he appears bewildered*). Where am I? (*He looks round.*) Ah! Yes; what is going on? (what is going on?)

CLERK (*handing him paper*). Here is your deposition — read it.

MATHIAS (*takes it and,* [*before reading it, aside*] *reading, crushes paper*). Wretched, wretched fool! [*I have told all; I am lost!*] (You've told all; you're lost!) (*With rage,* [*after reading the paper.*]) It is false! (*Tears the paper into pieces.*) You are a set of rogues! Christian — where is Christian? It is a crime against justice! They will not let my only witness speak. Christian! They would kill the father of your wife! Help me — help me! (Christian — why is he not here!)

PRESIDENT. [*You force me to speak of an event of which I had wished to remain silent.*] Your son-in-law Christian, upon hearing of the crimes with which you are charged, by his own hand sought his death. He is no more.

MATHIAS. Ah! (*He appears stupefied with dismay.*)

PRESIDENT (*after consulting the other* JUDGES, *rises, speaks in a solemn tone of voice*). Considering that on the night of the 24th December 1818, between midnight and one o'clock,

Mathias committed the crime of assassination upon the person of one Kovesky, and considering that this crime was committed under circumstances which aggravate its enormity — such as, premeditation, and for the purpose of highway robbery; the Court condemns the said Mathias to be hanged by the neck until he is dead!

(MATHIAS *staggers and falls on his knees — the* CROWD *make a movement of terror — the death-bell tolls — lights lowered gradually — then curtain at back of gauze descends, disclosing the scene as at commencement — lights up — Music, a peal of joy bells heard ringing.*)

CROWD (*without*). Annette! Annette! The bride!

(*Hurried steps are heard upon the stairs outside, and then a loud knocking at the door of the room.*)

CATHERINE (*without*). Mathias! Mathias! get up at once. It is late in the morning, and all our guests are below.

(*More knocking.*)

CHRISTIAN (*without*). *Mathias! Mathias!* (*Silence.*) How soundly he sleeps!

WALTER (*without*). Ho! Mathias, the wedding has commenced — Houp, houp! (*More knocking.*)

THE CROWD (*outside*). Burgomaster! Burgomaster! (*Loud knocking.*)

CATHERINE (*in an anxious voice*). He does not answer. It is strange. Mathias!

(*A discussion among many voices is heard without.*)

CHRISTIAN. No — it is useless. Leave it to me! (Stand away there.)

(*At the same moment several violent blows are struck upon the door, which falls into the room from its hinges. Enter* CHRISTIAN, *hurriedly — he runs to the alcove — Music, hurry.*)

CHRISTIAN. Mathias! (*Looks into alcove and staggers back into room.*) Ah!

(*Enter* CATHERINE *and* ANNETTE, *followed by* WALTER, HANS, *and the* CROWD, *all dressed for the wedding.*)

CATHERINE. What has happened, Christian, what has happened? (*She is rushing to alcove.*)

CHRISTIAN (*stopping her*). (Stand back —) Don't come near — don't come near.

CATHERINE (*endeavouring to pass*). I will see what it is. Let me pass; do not fear for me.

(MATHIAS *appears from the alcove — he is dressed in the same clothes as when he retired into the alcove at the commencement of the Scene, but his face is haggard, and ghastly pale — he comes out, his eyes fixed, his arms extended — as he rushes forward with uncertain steps, the* CROWD *fall back with horror, and form groups of consternation, with a general exclamation of terror.*)

MATHIAS [*in a voice of strangulation*]. The rope! the rope! Cut the rope!

(*He falls suddenly, and is caught in the arms of* HANS *and* WALTER, *who carry him to the chair in centre of stage — the Bells heard off — Music, the melody played in the Second Act when promise given — his hands clutch at his throat as if to remove something that strangles him.*)

MATHIAS (*in a voice of strangulation*). (Take the rope from my neck — take the rope from my neck!) (*He looks pitifully round as if trying to recognize those about him, and then his head falls on his breast —* CATHERINE, *kneeling, places her hand on* MATHIAS's *heart.*)

CATHERINE. Dead! (*The Bells cease.*)

(ANNETTE *bursts into tears — the* WOMEN *in the crowd kneel; the* MEN *remove their hats and bend their heads upon their breasts — tableau.*)

CURTAIN

[This Act of *The Bells* is printed here by kind permission of Messrs. Samuel French, Ltd., 26 Southampton Street, London, W.C.2, who publish the play.]

LOUIS THE ELEVENTH

SCENE: *The Throne Room in the Castle of Plessis les Tours*

Enter OLIVER, *door* C., DAUPHIN *and* CARDINAL

OLIVER (C.) My lord, our prayers are heard,
  The king revives.
DAUPHIN (R. C.) He lives!
OLIVER. His senses have return'd;
  With little help he thrice has tried to walk;
  There is great hope! he has desir'd this chamber
  May be clear'd. Prince, he would be alone.
DAUPHIN. But this affects not me — I am his son.
OLIVER (*up to* Dauphin). Alas! my lord; trust to my offices,
                                    (*Walks up stage.*)
  And he shall ask for you anon.
DAUPHIN. Accept my gratitude. (*Exeunt* DAUPHIN *and*
  CARDINAL, *door* R.)

  (*Enter* COMINES *and* TRISTAN, *door* R. *They stop and
  bow as the* DAUPHIN *and* CARDINAL *pass them.*)

TRISTAN. We are alone!
COMINES. Well.
TRISTAN. Will he live?
OLIVER. 'Tis doubtful still.
COMINES. Speaks he of Nemours?
OLIVER. No; he forgets.
COMINES. Nemours's condemned to death, and Coitier, too.
OLIVER. His brain is gone. (*Crosses to L. C. between them.*)
  Just now, why nought would serve him, but he must
  Preside at council; on his haggard brow
  I needs must place the crown, though with the weight
  His wizen'd chin sank down upon his breast;
  And o'er his ague-stricken form he wears
  The royal mantle; then he will walk, forsooth,

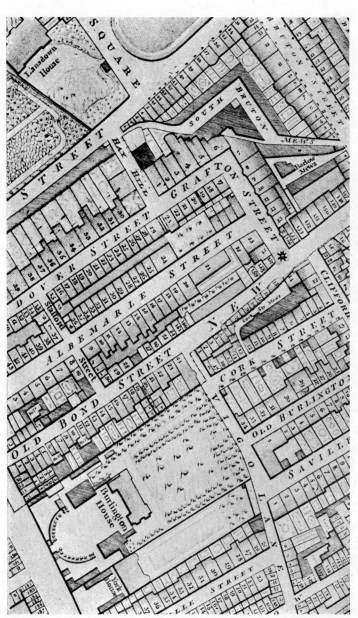

Plan showing the house, 15a Grafton Street, in which Irving lived from 1872 to 1899 . . . marked by a star. It also shows the house of Bancroft, Irving's friend, in Berkeley Square. From Horwood's plan of London, 1792–99.

But scarce has made one pace, when, breathless, helpless,
He sinks back, crying, " that he never felt so well."   Hush!
He comes.

(*Enter* Louis, *C. from L., two Attendants following C.
from L.*)

TRISTAN.   Has such a phantom life?

LOUIS.   What men are those?

OLIVER.   Tristan — Comines.

LOUIS (*peevish*).   Think you I cannot see 'em;
One would suppose my eyes were failing me.
Good day, sirs.   (*He falls forward and they support him.*)
Let go your hold!
Can I not stir without ye?   (*Sits.*)

(OLIVER *signs them to retire.   Servants exeunt L. H. D.*)

OLIVER.   There, repose — rest you awhile, Sire.

LOUIS.   I am not weary.

OLIVER.   No.

LOUIS.   I am strong and capable.

OLIVER.   Most capable.

LOUIS.   Since you will have it so. (*Gazing at* TRISTAN.)
Why stands he there, and gazes on me so?
Does he find me chang'd?

TRISTAN.   *I,* Sire?   I never saw you look so hale.

LOUIS.   That's well! — this room is spacious — there is air in't
— I can breathe — so — so.

OLIVER (*crosses round to L. C.*).   He sleeps.

(*All three come L.*)

COMINES.   Remember, gentlemen, he bade us once,
When his last moments came, to warn him.

TRISTAN.   He did.
Who shall tell him?
It must be done by one who can convey
The matter tenderly.   You are the man.   (*To* OLIVER.)

COMINES.   The very man, indeed.

OLIVER. I would accept, but, faith, I love him so,
I could not keep my feelings in command.
It must be firmly done, and you, I think,
Would do it best of all. (*To* COMINES.)

TRISTAN. He's right.

COMINES. I am willing; but why thus prolong
His woe? 'Twere better and more merciful
To speak outright and break the truth
At once, as you would do. (*To* TRISTAN.)

OLIVER. Why, so it would.

TRISTAN. Eh, gentlemen?
Let us confess — the thing is delicate.

(*Crosses between them.*)

LOUIS. Why do ye whisper there?

(*They start and turn slowly to him.*)

OLIVER. We bless the day for your recovery.

LOUIS. Why is not Coitier here?
Where does he lag? — go, fetch him.

TRISTAN (*crosses to L. C.*). Sire — you know.

LOUIS. I know! — I know he never is where I
Would have him be.

TRISTAN. But, Sire, you bade —

LOUIS. Away! I bade you bring him here — no words.
Obey. (*Exit* TRISTAN *R. H. door.* LOUIS *rises.*)
I feel in cue for hearty exercise.
Bid my Grand Equerry have the train
In readiness.
I'll take a gallop through the forest,
I'll try the full on the crook'd back o' Richard.

OLIVER (*R. H.*) How! Sire?

LOUIS. I'll hunt the wolf today.

(*Crosses C., then to L. and back to C.*)

OLIVER. But, Sire —

LOUIS. Begone! begone!

(OLIVER *goes up and exits door L. H.*)

My crown.
Why have they thrust it on me? Place it there,
Nearer — nearer still — beneath my eyes —
Under my hand. (COITIER *off R. I.*)

(COMINES *places the crown on table as* LOUIS *directs.*)
(*Enter* COITIER *and* TRISTAN, *R. H. door.*)

COITIER (*coming down L. C.*). From *my* lips he shall learn
what *you* so fear
To tell. (*Coming down L. C.*)
LOUIS. Ah! Coitier, art thou there — whence came ye?
COITIER. Whence! This is too much.
Whence came I? You are merry, Sire.
LOUIS. Why?
COITIER. Look on my wrist, still blushing with the rust
Your manacles have left there — whence come I!
Job's patience! — from a dungeon.
LOUIS. A dungeon — thou! Who gave the order?
COITIER. Who? You.
LOUIS. I?
COITIER. 'Fore heaven! he will deny it, now.
You in my presence gave it.
LOUIS. Where? — For what?
COITIER. Accuse me of a deed so vile. Why, Sire,
Had I the stomach for it, what hinder'd me?
A drug? — a remedy o'ercharg'd —
One drop too much, and I had done with ye!
But introduce a midnight murderer,
While ye were sleeping —
LOUIS (*rising*). Hold! hold! That vision —
In the night — behind those curtains — said ye?
COMINES. Coitier, what have you done?
LOUIS. No, no; I do remember, how;
'Twas he. Nemours! Nemours a dagger rais'd
Against my life. (*To* TRISTAN.) He's dead?
TRISTAN. I waited, Sire —

LOUIS.   Not dead?

COITIER (*coming down a little*).   Sire! think not on such de-
signs;
  Have done with vengeance; look to your own affairs.
  Your hour is come.

LOUIS (*staggers back to couch*).   Eh!

COITIER.   Look well, I say, to what you do,
  For, by the light of heaven, this day
  Will be your last!

LOUIS.   If so, it shall be also his.   Tristan,
  (TRISTAN *up a little, L. C.*)   Nemours, let him be executed
  Now, at once; no juggling with me,
  Or your own head shall answer it — begone!

COMINES.   Tristan! were it not well to wait.

TRISTAN.   My life or his — you hear — I have no choice.

(*Exit door R. H.   COITIER gets round to R. of table.*)

LOUIS.   My blood grows chill —
  Deserts my limbs, and gathers round my heart.
  Nay, this is weakness, but a spasm; 'twill pass —
  (COITIER *takes handkerchief from pocket.*)
  'Twill pass —— so wipe my brow! it is the sweat
  Of agony, and not the dews of death.
  Ah! now it comes; ay, go — the Dauphin —
  Quick.

COMINES.   (*Going up C.*)

LOUIS.   No; come back:
  If thus he saw me, he would believe 'twas past
  And over with me.   Oh! look not so, sirs,
  This is mere pain — not death; it cannot be.
  Save me, Coitier; oh! give me air — air — air —
  Oh! all my treasure for one breath — take — take;
  But save me — quick — 'tis not death — 'tis not!

(*Falls senseless on couch.*)

COITIER.   Go! Tell the Dauphin
  He is King of France, (*Exit COMINES door R. H.*)
  These sunken lips, and sightless, glazed eyes,

Bear witness of the livid seal of death. —
He's gone.

(*Examines the face of* Louis. *Raises his arm, and lets it fall.*)

And Nemours — Nemours is sav'd, sav'd.

Enter the Dauphin, Comines, *Lords, R. H. door.*

Coitier.   He is no more.
Dauphin.   Am I too late?   I would be alone.

(*Nobles bow.   All retire, door R. H.*)

Oh! my father!   (*Kneeling beside Couch.*)
This poor cold hand of thine, which now I seek
To warm with tears — 'tis
Death that gives me leave to kiss it thus.
Cold and incapable.   (*Places his hand on Crown.*)
This fatal bauble stood between our hearts —
Symbol of earthly power —

(Marie *rushes in, door R. H.*)

Marie.   My liege —
Dauphin.   Marie!
Marie.   He is condemned, Sire, Tristan is at
His bloody work!   Stay, stay it, Sire;
I claim your royal word — this ring —
I ask the pardon of Nemours — his life —
His life or mine — they lead him out to death!

(Louis, *during this, has shown signs of returning life; his first movement is to search for the Crown with his hand; rising and leaning on the table, regards the* Dauphin *and* Marie *with a haggard look.*)

Dauphin.   The King redeems the Dauphin's word —
Nemours —

(Louis *drags himself forward, and places his hand on the* Dauphin's *shoulder, who utters a cry of terror, and falls*

at MARIE's *feet, offering back the crown to his father;*
MARIE *strikes bell on table* R. C.—*Court enters slowly* R.)

LOUIS. *My hour is come!* (*Sinks in chair.*)
Approach and look upon me — here, I yield
The crown to him.
Mercy — for me — ask —
Pray — for mercy!

MARIE. Nemours — one word for him.

FRA. You hear.

MARIE (*kneeling*). My liege — my liege — as thou
dost hope for pardon,
Extend it now! (*Bell sounds.*)

DAUPHIN (*rises*). One word, my father — speak and give him
life.

FRA. Sire — while thou yet hast time.

LOUIS. If I forgive,
Shall I, in my turn, be forgiven?

FRA. Would'st thou contract with heaven,
And die accurs'd, as thou hast liv'd?

LOUIS. No, no, I pardon. Save him, save him.

(MARIE *rushes out, door* L. H. *Bell.*)

My father, speak. Speak words of comfort.
Wrap my freezing soul in hope. Absolve. Absolve.
Pray for my life to come. Oh, I repent.
I do repent. Save me.

COITIER. My liege,
Receive his breath, it is his last.

LOUIS. It comes, the mortal foe!
See, see you not it comes.
I feel his icy grip — pray — pray for me.
I do entreat ye all.
I command.

(*Endeavours to rise — falls forward dead.*)

FRA. and LORDS. The King is dead.
Long live the King.

CURTAIN

THE LYONS MAIL

ACT III, SCENE III

SCENE: *A room and balcony on the first floor of a wine shop at the corner of the Place de Grève. In the distance are seen the quay, and the Church of Notre Dame. Large door L.; a table and chair up R. C. The distant murmurs of the crowd are heard all through this scene.* DUBOSC *discovered seated drinking. Church clock strikes ten.*

DUBOSC. Ten o'clock. Not much sign of business yet. Only the crowd about the scaffold. My head won't be safe till that other fellow's rolls in the soup. (*Murmur. Noise of soldiers' drums.*) Soldiers! Business at last!

(FOUINARD[1] *slowly puts his head round door L.*)

FOUINARD (*watching him aside*). There he is! I'm afraid to go near him. (FOUINARD *enters slowly.*) Dubosc, Dubosc, I've something to tell you.

DUBOSC. Well, tell it like a man, don't wriggle there like an eel.

FOUINARD. Well, I'll tell you.

DUBOSC. Well, out with it — out with it. You white livered hound! (*Drinking.*)

FOUINARD. M. Dorval, the magistrate, drove off at full gallop from the prison, to get a respite for one of them.

DUBOSC. Which one — Lesurques?

FOUINARD. Yes.

DUBOSC. Damnation! (*Looks at him.*)

FOUINARD. Don't look at me like that; you have nothing to fear. The lawyers would cut off a hundred innocent heads — rather than own themselves mistaken. They say a woman has been wounded in that house — we — you know!

DUBOSC. Yes, I know. Janette!

FOUINARD. What, Janette!

---

[1] Acted by old John Archer, and acted excellently well.

DUBOSC. The only woman I ever loved. (*Drinks.*) Get me some *more brandy.* (*Drums.*)

FOUINARD. No, no: Dubosc, you've had enough already!

DUBOSC. Get me *some more brandy.*

FOUINARD. I wouldn't have any more brandy, Dubosc. You've had enough.

DUBOSC. I'm the best judge of that. *Get me some more brandy.* Will that cart never come? This is trifling with the public! Now if you're going to bring the cart, bring the cart along. I've been waiting here quite long enough! "*Allons enfants de la Patrie. Le jour de gloire est arrivé.*"

FOUINARD. Dubosc, do come away from that window; if they should see you, we are both lost.

DUBOSC. Don't be frightened my little Buonaparte — Buonaparte — etc., etc.

FOUINARD. Don't, don't, Dubosc. Besides Lesurques will be executed all in good time without your looking on. Poor Lesurques.

DUBOSC. Hullo, hullo, on whose side are you? Eh?

FOUINARD. On yours, Dubosc.

DUBOSC. Oh, you're on my side are you? Don't you wish I was in his place?

FOUINARD. No, no, Dubosc. No.

DUBOSC. Swear it, swear it, swear it! (DUBOSC *hits* FOUINARD *who falls R. C. head.* DUBOSC *kicks him.*) Get up you white livered hound you. Get up! Fetch me some more brandy or I'll tickle you again.

FOUINARD (*rises, gets bottle from table*). I'll fetch it Dubosc, as soon as I can.

DUBOSC. Go then, you white livered hound!

FOUINARD (*aside*). And I'll fetch something else that you don't reckon upon. (*Exit.*)

(*The murmur which has been going on all the scene, grows louder — this attracts* DUBOSC's *attention — He goes up stage.*)

DUBOSC. There they are, there they are! The cart at last. There's Choppard, there's Courriol, and there's the fellow they say is so like me. You're almost at home now, my gentlemen. Gee whoa! Gee whoa! Get on, you brutes. Stand aside, stand aside, and let the cart come on. At last! At last! They're mounting the scaffold at last! (*Murmurs suddenly cease.*) Damn that fellow. Why don't he bring the brandy. Oh, indeed, they're favouring the crowd with their last dying speech. (*Murmur starts again.*) No, they're not. Why it's Janette. Janette spouting. (*Murmur louder.*) Curse me, if the people and soldiers aren't mixing together. (*Crowd yells.*) Why there's Fouinard. Fouinard too. Has the beast turned traitor? (*Crowd shouting name " Dubosc."*) My name! They're pointing here! They're speaking of me. Nabbed — nabbed at last, but they shan't have me cheap! (*Locks door. Business at window and door. Undoes the door on the inside which swings back on and up stage, allowing* DUBOSC *to get through trick door.*)

(*Quick change to Lesurques.*)

(*When the door is burst open, enter* COMMISSARY *and* FOUR GENDARMES, *followed by* CROWD, FOUINARD *and* JANETTE. *They look round, see* DUBOSC *behind door. He rushes up towards window, but is seized from behind and bound by the* GENDARMES. *A joyful shout is heard off L. The Crowd divided, and enter* LESURQUES, JULIE, DIDIER, JEROME, LAMBERT, GUERNEAU, DORVAL, *and* FRIENDS. *The shout is taken up by those on the stage and kept on till finish.*) (*Tableaux.*)

CURTAIN

(Sir John Martin Harvey holds the rights of this play, and has generously allowed me to reprint this scene.)

AND NOW you are wondering why, to the great actor of genius, stuff like this is preferable to better-written stuff which you, I, and also the great actor will admit is better stuff.

" Why is this so ? " I asked of the Great Actor,[1] imagining him present. And I gathered that this was his reply:

" It is an exaggeration to say that a well-written play, like *The School for Scandal,* for example, is not playable by sixteen good actors, even as it would be an exaggeration to say that a good symphony, like Tchaikowski's No. 6, is not playable by a good orchestra of musicians. The good actor is like a good instrumentalist. But in these cases, the whole matter turns round *Ensemble.*

" So much for the good actors. But now of the great actor.

" The great actor and the very able actor are two different breeds. There are never sixteen great actors on a stage together, though there may be sixteen able actors. Theoretically, no actor can be more than a first-rate actor; practically, the exception proves this rule. I am what is called a great actor — and some hold me to be a somewhat disturbing person — one who is often very good and often (so they hold) very bad. Theoretically, it is better to have all actors steadily good than fitfully wonderful, and the reverse — because with sixteen steadily good actors (could we find them) we should have a group who could interpret any very good play, well-constructed and well-written — and this would undoubtedly be a blessing, as

[1] Not Irving, but the personification of the great actors of any time.

are all ideals. But however grand this ideal may be in theory, it is seldom if ever realized. There should be sufficient room in any city for a theatre which boasts a group of good actors, and for a theatre with an actor of genius as the sole attraction. What a lucky public that would be which could boast of possessing both.

"Both the group and the individual genius would have their partisans, who would attempt to spoil the fun by creating a rivalry which was not evident, and would try to prevent the general public from enjoying both. While the individual Irving worked in London, Mr. John Hare with the Kendalls and other fine comedians formed a first-rate group. The partisans, as ever, tried to stir up bad feeling; but London, too big to be bothered, had the benefit of both, and appreciated both.

"But Genius and *Ensemble* never mix well — never move alike, or along the same paths: their trains of thought are in direct opposition. While I appreciate groups, I cannot work with them. Offer *The School for Scandal* to an actor of genius — to me — and my first words after reading it will be: I can't play *Sir Peter* and *Joseph* and *Charles* and *Sir Oliver* — *there is no part for me in this play*.

"On hearing this you will think it is confounded conceit on my part to speak so — and you are wrong. You ask me what I mean, and I offend you by the next answer, which is that there isn't a big enough part for me.

"That thoroughly enrages you — but give the thing a little quiet thought and, if possible, see what I mean. I mean this: I am an accursed genius — what? — obliged to work alone; and the nature of every genius prevents him from being a scrap of good when asked to do his level best and no more — for he hasn't a *level best*. He is all fits and starts — that's me. I'm a tree, not a lot of cut flowers. Put a tree in a delicate vase, and it will burst it . . . this can't be helped — but don't blame the tree for its power, blame the vase for its fragility.

"So it is with me — put me in a play like *The School for Scandal* or Tchekov's *Three Sisters,* and I shall spoil it: and it's useless for me to spend my life cursing fate which has made me so; I'm different from the others — can't be helped. I might complain —

Oh why was I born with a different face?
Why was I not born like the rest of my race?
When I look each one starts, when I speak I offend,
Then I'm silent and passive, and lose every friend.

but what is the use of complaining — far better rejoice that the public is happy that I exist.

"You see what I mean: when passive, as a good actor should be, I lose all touch — I am no one. That's why I look for a part which is *active* — a part which, like a vivid personality in real life, seems to have the stage to itself — is only sketched in by the playwriter — leaves me much to do, to imagine, to invent. It is my only chance — do you wish to rob me of that? Do so, and you rob yourselves.

"Now do you understand when I say that there is no part for me in *The School for Scandal?* If I play *Sir*

Peter as though it were a rôle which requires a blazing genius, I ruin the admirable play — I break the delicate vase. And that's the only way I can play any part — and this is why I said just now that there isn't a big enough part for me in that play; at which you thought me a vain fool. You see I know myself; and I shall thank goodness if the public does me the courtesy of appreciating this fact.

" Now the next point is, what kind of part *is* big enough for me. And the reply is: that kind of part which leaves me free — which leaves me plenty of room in which to display my genius . . . leaves half undone till I do it.

" You ask if *Hamlet, Macbeth, Othello* and *Lear* will serve. I reply that these do offer me plenty of room, but do not leave me free — although I will admit that I and other actors of genius have made free with the rôles. Whether I am strictly right in doing so, is neither here nor there: I do it — having done so, I may admit, with the smile of the successful thief, that I proceeded not exactly according to the strictest rules of the immaculate conscience. I did as I should not have done, in preference to parading as a patron of little prejudices. I regret rolling these four p's off on the tip of my tongue: I have no genius for phrases, and so I should not indulge. But I am on to my theme, and I cannot stop.

" *Hamlet* and *Lear* having suffered at my hands, it is only natural that in my calmer moments I should realize that, for a display of my powers, in place of a great play a dummy is any day better. *Hamlet* and *Lear* went down before me in the first round — and what you want is not to see me lay out my opponent quite so early, for then the fun is over. You want to see me in twelve rounds: good — then give me a dummy. I put it crudely, for you yourselves have said that

> *I'm either too low or too highly priz'd,*
> *When elate I'm envied; when meek I'm despis'd.*

For a boxer to knock out his antagonist too early in the match, is to cheat you of a fight — but for an actor to wipe the floor with his very collaborator — with Shakespeare — even he — and to do so in the first round, is even worse than that. So you must allow the actor of genius to select a rôle and a play which he can count on as offering sufficient *resistance*.

"The toughest, the least literary play does this — a play of mere bones strung together, without subtleties, without complexes. The story must be clear, and not more than one story must be told in the same play. *The Merchant of Venice* is the weaker for its second story about *Portia* — it is the tale of *Shylock* that was wanted. Still, we great actors can manage, as you have seen, to get round that — we cut *Portia's* tale to ribbons, and on we go.

"But we are not so happy doing that, and you must at least credit us with the possession of conscience in that matter: we know what it is we are doing — we stifle our conscience, and go on.

"So we actors of genius really prefer a play that is not a great play. For example, Frédéric Lemaître, one of us,

Henry Irving as Mephistopheles — Act II, "Faust." Drawn by
Paul Renouard. *From the Collection of Mr. James Carew.*

took *L'Auberge des Adrets,* which was a sinister little drama, a plain-sailing trifle, such as went down with the public — went down in the strict sense of the words, as a ship sinks and is lost for ever: but Lemaître rigged it out anew, and it came sailing in as though it were a Spanish Galleon. Paris was astounded. Whether right or wrong — he was right.

"But you do not like my example, maybe. Let us take a finer one — in a finer art, too — let us take Mozart. When he would show off (and after all, you will say that this is what we great actors do — no more) — when he would show off, then, did he select a piece by Haydn or Palestrina or the great Brune (who I suspect was really plain Brown), or did he pick out some little nothing of a tune? He did the latter — playing it once over as written, to show how simple it was, he then started in to do what Lemaître did — he turned it inside out; he elaborated here and there and here again, and everyone marvelled at his improvisation. Believe me, what Mozart did, we too may do. It is just this, and there is no argument that can be advanced to disallow it."

IT was at this point, as I was recording these words, I stopped short — paused to think — though for quite a long time — determined not to reveal a thing that was then passing through my mind — put down my pen — looked up — and saw Irving before me.

You must not think I exaggerate. I was alone — the wind, 'tis true, was howling down the valley outside my house — how it howwwled! — yet all was cosy and well

lit in my room — nothing dusky, nothing weird: yet there
— there stood Irving.

Perhaps you have never seen a spirit. It is impossible
for me to pass a week without seeing one — but then, I
make no effort to raise a spirit — one is there — or there
— and here was Irving . . . a kind of apparition — yes,
that was it — and a kind voice saying, " Well, my boy,
fiddling with a pen — what ? "

I said not a word. Anon I rose up automatically, to
vacate the only chair.

" That's all right, my boy . . . writing (and he was
grinning gently), writing is ever an exhausting ex-er-cise.
For my part — I — er — seldom wrote."

He came a step nearer: it was strange, for he seemed
to telescope out slightly in all directions.

" I know what it is you have written," he went on.
" These papers here, my boy — very excellent — highly
flattering too, I'm sure — do a great deal of good." He
broke off abruptly. . . " What do you intend to call the
book ? "

" Well, sir, I thought to call it ' *On Henry Irving.*' "

There was a long pause: Irving took a few steps in the
direction of the south wall of my room, and said, " Why
not ' *On George Bernard Shaw* '? "

This slightly embarrassed me, for I thought I had been
devoting myself entirely to one subject — that is to say,
to Irving — and I felt as small as I always had done thirty-
odd years ago, when he was speaking.

" But there is so little about Mr. Shaw in this book. . ."

" Damn sight too much," said Irving, wheeling round

noiselessly and in a flash, and looking precisely as he used to look when he held four thousand people silent: even if a zany should have run across the stage, making grimaces, still he would have held them silent; therefore, I would ask you to be silent now.

"Cut it out, my boy," he then said, moving a long finger many times over the manuscript. "Cut it out. . . Advertising the Advertiser."

I don't know how many hours passed, as I stopped to think of the significance of what he had said, and the importance of doing as he wished. But when you have a loved familiar spirit, you need not fear that he is going to vanish. He will hold the attitude, and pick up his discourse exactly where he left it off ten hours or ten days ago, if your familiar spirit is really a white-winged angel. (You see, we have got back to it after all, and Laurence knew we should.)

But Irving off the earth is more extraordinary still than Irving on the stage. He is devoid of all those worldly-wise little prejudices which so many misunderstood while he was alive (for example, that prejudice in favour of living, rather than dying): and Irving off the earth adds more than a cubit to even his stature . . . though he has one prejudice, that of doing anything rather than live again.

So that whereas while living, he would have prevented any reference to Mr. Shaw, he added after the long pause to which I have just referred: "but perhaps nec-ess-ary. As I see it now," he said, "that man has done a very great harm to my beloved profession. Among other things, he has taught Dramatic Critics to hold the Theatre in contempt. The — er — queer things that you, my boy, say in your books " — and he ran the back of his finger-nail along a row of my own publications, " are what in London we used to call somewhat rash — yes, rash. Once I might have called them im-per-ti-nent: the opinions expressed therein are very open to — er — censure." Here he ran his finger again along the backs of my books: " poss-ibly unread except by thirty or forty jackasses in England. But you, my dear Ted, always loved the Theatre: I have watched you, and I know it. I think, too, you have always loved the actor." (And here I could see that he meant one actor.) " But the actors seem to have . . . " — a slight movement of the hand — another faint motion — a pause — " vanished. . .

" A rev-er-ence, let alone anything deeper, for our calling was essential in an actor, and — I think . . . er — will always be — essential. . . To perform in a play by a man who despises our sacred calling " . . . well-controlled passion lent his voice a strange vibration . . . " countenance the Shaws, and soon we shall have the priests kissing the hem of Satan: I think I put it precisely? A good man, doubtless . . . kind to his wife — let us hope — but a damned evil to the theatrical profession of Great Britain: because a man of brains and ca-pa-ci-ty."

A long pause. Irving was walking up and down. Suddenly he stopped. " You had better say this, my boy. It will do a little harm: it may do con-sid-er-able good. I was never a very great, or shall I say, a very ri-ot-ous propagandist. Queen Victoria, the sainted lady, who I

EPILOGUE 225

am glad to see is still as deeply loved, even by the younger writers of the time, as she was by those of us who may today be called Victorians — Queen Victoria was a noble lady . . . profoundly religious . . . and therefore, na-tu-ra-lly, devoted to the Theatre. Er — yes: by the bye, I see you have been knighted, my boy — very good — very good."

I protested that I had not been knighted. "Not knighted — but it's in the papers!"

"No, Henry," I said (and he seemed to like being called "Henry" again). "That was somebody else."

"Really — most interesting — in my time, there were two Henry Irvings besides myself — I'm not referring to Harry: and now you have another Edward Gordon Craig in the world?"

"No," I said, "an Ernest Gordon Craig."

"Ah! Ernest — Ernest," repeated Irving — "Wilde pointed to the er-r — importance of that. The importance of earnestness, if you have the time for it" — and here he looked odd and quizzical, "is not to be overrated. The theatrical profession today is not so earnest as I should like to see it. There is not enough enthusiasm among the men of the Theatre."

I said, "Well, you see, it is a curious thing, but enthusiasm today is held to be rather bad form."

"Oh, bad form, is it?" said Irving, in cutting and vibrating tones . . . "bad form to believe in God Almighty, is it? . . . A pity," he added, and continued to walk up and down the room, murmuring ". . . a pity. . . . There was a young spark in the Victorian era . . .

Benjamin Disraeli. It interests me to note that most
of the modern literature of the young men of today
is based upon this young spark's trifles. Well, this young
scamp, in one of his books, has an excellent passage:
'*Never apologize for showing enthusiasm, my friend.
Remember that when you do so, you apologize for
truth.*'" Irving had deliberately put the word "enthusiasm" in place of "feeling."

"Intensity of feeling, enthusiasm, power, these of course
come from a — rmm — Victorian sense of belief. And
from enthusiasm spring fine manners. Manners and
enthusiasm are not divided: this is seldom sufficiently
realized — and it is a very important point. The bad manners of the London managers in handling their theatres
as though they were shops, is a little point which I see
you have touched on once or twice in your writings.
Touch on it again."

Irving paused in his walk, suddenly: "Of course, in my
day, when we had arrived at a position of authority, we
had but to mention a thing quietly for it to be noted —
and for something to be done. But I observe that today
you have to bawl to be heard. Well, bawl, my dear boy,
bawl, but mention it. The bad manners in our Theatre
have to cease — the enthusiasm to increase. The — er
— loy-al-ty of all to all should become more marked.
Glad to see," he said, turning round, "that you boys at the
Lyceum are all loyal to each other. And now for a
fatal thing:" he repeated the word three times — "fatal
. . . fatal. I refer to the long runs. Yes, my own runs
were long, but not to the extended length that yours are

today. Nice little plays, these of today, and pleasantly performed, but not exactly worthy of long runs. Furthermore — er-r — you have among you — certain rogues" (those who knew Irving will remember the strange, quiet, and sinister way in which he uttered the word "rogues") "certain rogues," he repeated, "who, pretending to save the English Theatre — calling themselves artists — God save the mark! — come before the respected public of England, and offer it what can only be described as t r a s h."

His voice had become almost hushed, so furious was he. The whole face, the skin of it, drawn, like a drum that you can see being tightened by the player. He looked no less noble than before, but you could see that fury was raging within him.

He said, "This is the lowest crime that can be committed upon the body of our noble Theatre."

Then his mood instantly changed. "And what do you do for a living, my dear Ted?" he asked. "Oh, I write books, and make woodcuts, and—" "But," he interrupted, "you're a very celebrated man in the theatrical profession — no? . . . a kind of leader, what?"

Here the cock crew.

Irving was moving slowly towards the door: and as he turned the handle—"A leader?" I answered; "perhaps some day, when I have as good followers as you have."

He paused . . . looked long and fixedly at me, and then moved on: "Well, good-bye," he said — that gentle motion with his hand — and, "Good-bye . . . Good-bye."

INDEX